The Mature Student's Study Guide

If you want to know how . . .

A Practical Guide to Research Methods
A user-friendly guide to mastering research techniques and projects

Writing Your Dissertation
*The best-selling guide to planning, preparing and
presenting first-class work*

Writing an Assignment
Proven techniques from a chief examiner that really get results

Critical Thinking for Students
Learn the skills of critical assessment and effective argument

howtobooks

For full details, please send for a free copy
of the latest catalogue to:

How To Books
Spring Hill House, Spring Hill Road, Begbroke
Oxford OX5 1RX, United Kingdom
email: info@howtobooks.co.uk
www.howtobooks.co.uk

Dr Catherine Dawson

The Mature Student's Study Guide

Essential skills for those returning to education or distance learning

howtobooks

Published by How To Books Ltd,
Spring Hill House, Spring Hill Road, Begbroke,
Oxford OX5 1RX, United Kingdom.
Tel: (01865) 375794. Fax: (01865) 379162.
Email: info@howtobooks.co.uk
http://www.howtobooks.co.uk

First published 2004
Second edition 2006

British Library Cataloguing in Publication Data.
A catalogue record for this book is available from
the British Library.

ISBN 10: 1 84528 124 1
ISBN 13: 978 1 84528 124 3

Produced for How To Books by Deer Park Productions, Tavistock
Typeset by Kestrel Data, Exeter, Devon
Cover design by Baseline Arts Ltd, Oxford
Printed and bound by Cromwell Press Ltd, Trowbridge, Wiltshire

NOTE: The material contained in this book is set out in good
faith for general guidance and no liability can be accepted
for loss or expense incurred as a result of relying in particular
circumstances on statements made in the book. Laws and
regulations are complex and liable to change, and readers should
check the current position with the relevant authorities before
making personal arrangements.

Contents

List of Tables

Preface

This book has been written for adults who are worried or anxious about their ability to study effectively. It is aimed at adults in all types of education, from short courses to degree length courses, in further education colleges, universities or within adult education institutions. It will also be of use to adults studying through open, distance or technology enabled learning (e-learning).

This book provides advice and guidance on all aspects of study, from improving writing skills to passing examinations. The information is presented in a clear, accessible way which allows you to dip into the relevant chapters whenever you feel the need to improve certain study skills. As such, it is a practical handbook which will be of use throughout your studies.

As an adult you may find that studying puts extra demands on you, both physically and emotionally. Perhaps you are trying to study while holding down a full-time job, or you may be trying to juggle family responsibilities with study. This book acknowledges the fact that adults face extra pressures, and provides advice and guidance on how to cope with this while studying.

I have been a researcher and tutor working with adult learners for over nineteen years. My experiences have helped me to put together this book with adults' hopes, fears, aspirations and goals at the forefront of its design and content. All the examples and quotations used in this book have been gathered over the last nineteen years and during the research for my doctorate.

I hope that you find this book interesting and useful and that you are able to refer to it often throughout your course. Good luck with your studies.

Catherine Dawson

(1)

Learning How to Learn

Many adults who have been out of the education system for some time are concerned about their ability to learn effectively. They worry that their brains have 'gone stale' or that you 'can't teach an old dog new tricks'. However, this is not the case. Anyone of any age has the capacity to learn – we all continue learning throughout our lives.

Yet, for your learning to be both efficient and effective, it is important to think first about *how* you learn. By doing this you will find that you understand your learning better, your studies become more enjoyable and you are able to learn more in less time. This chapter provides advice and guidance about learning *how* to learn.

WHAT IS 'LEARNING'?

Learning is not just about memorising facts. It also includes the development of skills, knowledge, critical thinking and power of argument. Learning also helps us to carry out tasks more successfully and more efficiently. Learning can be divided into three areas:

◆ Learning which helps you improve your physical abilities. At school you might have been taught how to play

1

netball, football or hockey. You might have had swimming lessons as a child. Indeed, as a very young child you learned how to stand, walk, run and hop.

◆ Learning which helps you to develop and increase your knowledge. Everything you know has been learned at some stage in your life.

◆ Learning which helps you to change your attitude and beliefs. This could be in a formal learning setting – you might have been taught something by a school teacher which made you change your mind about something in which you believed, or you may have experienced a situation that tested your existing assumptions, helped you to learn something new and changed your attitudes.

RECOGNISING PRIOR EXPERIENTIAL LEARNING

When we return to learning we carry with us all the baggage of our previous learning experiences. For some adults these experiences will be negative, whereas for others they may be positive. Most adults, however, will be able to draw on both positive and negative experiences, all of which can help you to evaluate and improve your learning.

It is important that you can learn from all your experiences, and, as an adult, you have a great deal of experience on which to draw. Experiences are not just about the acquisition of knowledge, but about the process through which you move to acquire this knowledge. For example, you may have tried to learn French at school but think that you were not very successful because you didn't pass your O Level or GCSE. However, you went through the *process* of learning a language, and as an adult you can draw on this learning experience. You might decide to learn Spanish because you go on frequent holidays to Spain – your motivation levels are much higher, you are interested in the language and you have your school experiences on which to draw. All this should contribute towards a positive learning experience.

If you are new to your subject area, you may think that you have no knowledge of your subject. However, you almost certainly will have some knowledge, although you may not have recognised this. Your interest in the subject must have developed from somewhere – perhaps it was a television programme or a newspaper article. If this is the case you will have information about the subject stored somewhere in your memory. As your course progresses, you will find that this previously stored knowledge filters through into your studies and helps you with your reading and essay writing.

EVALUATING YOUR PRIOR LEARNING

To help you think about your ability to learn, think about all the times when learning has been successful and all the times when learning has been unsuccessful. Table 1 provides an example of this exercise from Alice, a 31-year-old mother of two, enrolled on an access course.

Alice was surprised to find that she had more items of successful learning than she had of unsuccessful learning, especially as she had considered herself to be a 'failure' at school.

SUCCESSFUL LEARNING	REASONS FOR SUCCESS
Passed driving test.	Good instructor; enjoy driving and need to drive.
Raised two children.	Love my children and want the best for them.
Remember telephone numbers and addresses.	Important to keep in contact with people; find it easy to remember names and numbers.
Passed secretarial course.	Needed to pass course to get a job; enjoyed college and had a good tutor.
Learned routines and processes at work.	Wanted to do well in my job; needed the money; enjoyed working at that place – made work easier and more comfortable when I knew what I was doing.
Obtained lifesaving badges.	Parents told me how important it was and paid for lessons; enjoyed swimming; knew it might save my life.
Passed Geography, Art, English and Biology O Levels.	Enjoyed the subjects; was good at art; liked the teachers.
UNSUCCESSFUL LEARNING	**REASONS FOR FAILURE**
Failed O Level Maths, Cookery and Needlework.	Found maths very hard. Didn't like cookery and needlework and was forced to take those subjects. Didn't like the teacher or the way she taught.
Tried to teach myself Spanish.	Lack of motivation; I was unconfident and I am not a good teacher!

Table 1. Evaluation of prior learning

From the above exercise it becomes clear that for successful learning to take place, the following should occur:

◆ The skills to be learned are relevant to you and your needs.

◆ You are interested in your learning.

◆ You are motivated to learn.

◆ You can learn to use these skills in different contexts and activities.

◆ You are actively involved in the learning process.

◆ You are able to think, develop and work at your own pace.

◆ You feel comfortable in your learning environment.

◆ You are comfortable with the instructor, teaching methods and/or teaching materials.

Learning can be unsuccessful for the following reasons and it is important to notice that some of these reasons are through no fault of your own:

◆ Poor teaching methods and/or materials.

◆ Uncomfortable learning environment.

◆ Lack of confidence.

◆ Low opinion of self and ability.

◆ Stress.

◆ Lack of motivation and interest.

◆ Irrelevance to life and interests.

◆ Forced to do something you don't want to do.

An important part of learning *how* to learn is the development of self-evaluation skills. It is useful to do this at the start of your course as it will help you to think about your prior experience in relation to the subjects you hope to study. However, it is useful to continue this self-evaluation throughout your course. One way to do this is through keeping a learning diary which is discussed in Chapter 3.

RECOGNISING YOUR LEARNING STYLE

Over recent years a great deal has been written about individual learning styles. Some people believe that the learning style you were born with remains the same throughout your life, whereas others believe learning styles can and will change as you grow older.

Today, on the internet, there are a variety of surveys which will help you to start thinking about your preferred learning style. Just type 'Learning Style Survey' into a search engine and see what comes up. I have tested two of these surveys and they are both fairly accurate in terms of my learning style. Have a go at filling them in – it's an interesting exercise because it makes you think about the way you retain information. However, you should remember that this type of online survey can be open to misinterpretation and error – don't take the results too seriously.

An awareness of your learning style may help to point you in the direction of the right course and could help to overcome problems you might experience due to a mismatch in teaching and learning styles. However, good tutors will recognise that people learn in different ways and they will tailor their teaching methods to the learning style and preferences of people in their class. If they don't do this, students will not enjoy their learning and find it an unfulfilling and dissatisfying experience. Often, older students perceive this to be a problem with their personal ability to learn, thinking that their brains are getting 'woolly' due to their age. However, this is not the case. Instead, problems such as this may arise because of the *teaching style of the tutor* and not because of your ability to learn.

When thinking about your learning style, it might help to ask yourself the following questions:

1) Do I prefer to work through problems myself or do I prefer to discuss them with other people?
2) Do I rush into solving a problem immediately, or do I prefer to sit back and think about all the options first?
3) Do I prefer practical experimentation or do I like to think about theoretical issues?
4) Do I try to be objective and detached or do I like to form relationships and share my personal opinions?
5) Do I prefer working with figures or words?
6) Do I like to be team-leader, led by others or work on my own?
7) Am I a good team-player? What role do I take within a team?

8) Do I like to read about an issue first, or discuss it first with other people?

9) What method of teaching did I most prefer at school? Why was this?

10) What method of teaching did I least prefer at school? Why was this?

11) Do I always believe what I am told or do I have to check it out for myself?

12) Do I think problems through step-by-step or do I prefer to view the whole picture?

13) Do I see a new situation as a challenge or as a barrier?

IMPROVING CONCENTRATION AND MEMORY

Everyone can improve their memory. Indeed, some people believe that there is no such thing as bad memory – instead people just use their memory badly.

Our memory is made up of two main parts – the short-term memory and the long-term memory. In the short-term memory we store facts and ideas for as long as we need to apply them. In the long-term memory we store information that we will use at a later stage. To pass information from the short-term memory to the long-term memory we have to practise what we have learned. This involves careful reflection and analysis, thinking about what we have learned, writing about the concepts and ideas and understanding them. It may also involve some form of repetition and rote learning, especially in the case of facts and figures.

There are four parts to developing an effective memory:

◆ Information is received through various ways – the eyes, ears, touch, smell and taste. However, to receive information effectively, we must be open to receiving the information. This means that the information we wish to receive must have some personal relevance and we must be paying attention to what we are receiving.

◆ The information is stored in our memory in an effective manner. This will depend upon the type of information we are receiving. Facts and figures may have to be repeated over and over again, ideas and concepts may have to be thought about, written about and discussed. The storage of information is more effective if we understand what we are storing.

◆ The information has to be stored in an appropriate place within our memory. This involves a process of organisation where ideas are related to each other. It is easier to remember things if we can relate it to past experience and knowledge.

◆ We must be able to retrieve effectively the information when it is required. This may involve practice in recalling information and regularly reviewing the information we have stored.

As we have seen earlier, people learn in different ways. This affects the way we remember. For example, some people will find it much easier to remember faces whereas others find it easier to remember names. Your memory can be improved by understanding the learning style which helps you to take in and retain information in the most effective way. If you consider multi-sensory modes of learning – including sight, sound and touch – interest is added to the learning process and information is retained more effectively. Research has shown that school children find it easier to learn if it is possible to see, hear, say and touch the relevant materials. Learning can also be enhanced by the use of movement, such as that found in dance and drama.

For adults, information retention can be enhanced with the use of auditory and visual modes of learning – for example, learning rhymes to help you remember, or using visual images such as videos and slides. Do you remember the colours of the rainbow through the name ROY G. BIV, do you sing the song, or do you use the phrase 'Richard of York gave battle in vain'? If you find the method that suits you, it will help your memory to become more efficient and effective.

Tips for Improving Memory

Understand thoroughly what is to be remembered. If in doubt discuss it with your tutor and/or other students.

Only remember important and useful facts verbatim. Don't waste time trying to memorise facts and figures that you will not use.

If you have to remember something verbatim, try remembering at different times, for example when you are doing the housework or collecting the children from school.

Try to study first the information you wish to retain the longest.

If you find it easier to think in pictures, try to represent the information graphically and then commit the image to memory. Some people find it useful to draw pictures, while others prefer to imagine them. A pictorial representation does not have to be realistic – often the more unusual, the easier it is to remember.

If the material is very important, over-learn to keep the information fresh in your mind and return to the information on several occasions.

Find an interest in the material to help you to remember.

If you think in words, make a list of key words and organise it in a way that is meaningful to yourself – this might be alphabetically or so that the words produce a story.

Make associations with the words – the stronger the association, the more you will remember.

Think of an acronym to help you remember – this is a word or a group of words made from a longer message. Because it is shorter, it is easier to remember. The acronym doesn't have to make sense – it just needs to work for you.

Think of a rhyme to help you remember. This method has been used for centuries.

> Discuss the idea with a friend or relative. Try explaining it out loud as this will help you to remember. Recitation in front of someone who can correct you is a useful way to aid memory.

TRAINING YOUR MIND TO LEARN

One of the most important parts of training your mind to learn is to recognise and take control of those factors that distract you from your learning. Chapters 2 and 3 consider environmental distractions and those caused by other people, but perhaps even more powerful are those influenced by our own minds and bodies. Examples of these distractions are listed in Table 2 below.

EMOTIONAL	PHYSICAL	PYSCHOLOGICAL	SOCIOLOGICAL
Lack of confidence	Mobility problems	Fear of failure	Unable to work in groups
Lack of motivation	Poor eyesight	Low self-esteem	Difficult to bond with fellow students
Lack of interest	Poor hearing	Deflated ego	No connection with tutor
Feelings of nervousness or anxiety	Health problems	Feelings of alienation or being 'out of place'	Unfamiliar learning environment

Table 2.   Learning distractions

Create a similar table and fill it with your personal distractions. Once you have recognised these distractions you will be able to resolve the problems by tackling them one at a time. Start with those that are easy to rectify such as having your eyesight and hearing checked. Other identifiable problems will decline or be reduced as your course progresses and you become more familiar and comfortable with the learning environment.

SUMMARY

This chapter has discussed the importance of learning how to learn. By understanding the way in which you learn you can begin to learn more efficiently. This will help you to learn more in less time and enable your studying to become more effective and successful. Learning includes the development of skills, knowledge, critical thinking and powers of argument. To help your learning you need to recognise and evaluate your prior learning and come to understand your individual learning style. Another key factor in the learning process is the ability to train your mind, improve your concentration and memory and keep yourself free from distraction.

The following chapter offers further advice on coping with distractions. It also discusses the issues of personal health and the importance of creating a comfortable study environment.

② Preparing for Study

For successful study to take place you need to prepare carefully. This includes emotional, psychological, physical and environmental preparation. In other words you need to adopt a constructive attitude with high levels of motivation, maintain your health and create a working space conducive to learning. This chapter provides advice on how to go about preparing yourself, and others around you, for study.

MAINTAINING HEALTH

You need to make sure that you maintain your health at levels suitable to aid your studies. This is not to say that people with poor health cannot study – of course they can. However, you need to make sure that your health does not have an adverse influence on your studies. As an adult you know the importance of diet, exercise and sleep. Don't let your studies take over your life so much that you neglect these activities – they are so important to your physical wellbeing.

You will be required to do a lot of reading during your studies, so remember to have your eyes tested on a regular basis. You may also need to have your hearing checked so that you can get the most out of lectures. If you have problems with your eyesight or hearing which will affect your studies, make contact with the Disability Officer at your college or university. This person will be able to help you by arranging for note-takers to accompany you to lectures, or by providing equipment such as dictating machines or text magnifiers (see Chapter 18).

CREATING A WORKING ENVIRONMENT

If you intend to study at home you need to create a working environment that will help, rather than hinder, your studies. This means that you need to have furniture and equipment that is comfortable and suits your style of working, and you will need to find a quiet space free from distractions. This can be hard for adults with family commitments, but it is advisable to try to establish some ground rules at the start of your studies so that you can avoid problems later on.

We don't all have the luxury of being able to afford new office equipment. However, if you follow the health and safety considerations listed in the box below, you will create a more comfortable and productive working environment. Well designed furniture that suits your body size can reduce pain and injury, increase productivity and improve your mood and morale. Suitable furniture can also help to eliminate awkward posture.

If possible you should use your working environment only for studying and for important paperwork. Items that are used for leisure, such as televisions or radios, should be kept away from your working environment. You need to be able to make a clear distinction between work and leisure time

Health and Safety Guidelines – Working Environment

Your chair should be at a height that allows a 90° angle at your elbows for typing.

You should be able to sit with your thighs horizontal, your lower legs vertical and your feet flat on the floor or on a footrest.

The seat should swivel and have a padded, curved seat.

The back of the chair should offer firm support and you should be able to sit upright with your back on the lumbar support without the seat cutting into the back of your knees.

You should allow plenty of legroom.

Your desk needs to be big enough to allow for all your computing equipment and provide space for your paper-work.

You should keep frequently used items within easy reach.

The top of your computer screen should be at eye-level or slightly lower.

The viewing distance of your screen should be 45–60 cm (18–24 inches).

You should make sure that your mouse is placed level with your keyboard and near enough so that you don't have to stretch.

You need to make sure that there is enough light – natural daylight is best, but if you intend to work during the evenings make sure that you have good lighting that does not produce glare or shadows on your books, paper or screen.

The room should have good, natural ventilation.

and if you have a separate working space you will find this much easier to do.

BUILDING AND IMPROVING MOTIVATION

My personal experience suggests that adult learners, in general, tend to be more motivated than younger students in their studies. This is probably because adults have invested more in the learning process, not just in financial terms, but also in the way that returning to learning influences their lives, their attitudes, their families, their employment prospects and their psychological wellbeing. For many adults, returning to education is a huge decision that cannot be taken lightly. Once they have decided that this is the right option for them, they are determined to do well and show that they are capable of succeeding. These attitudes serve to keep motivation levels high.

REASON FOR POOR MOTIVATION	COPING STRATEGY
Lack of family support – conflict makes it hard to remain motivated, no help from family members with housework.	Discussed reasons for enrolling on course with family. Showed that it would benefit whole family. Pointed out that it would not be for ever. Asked for help.
Arguments about financial problems. Worrying about lack of money.	Visited Student Support Officer and received a hardship grant.
Course was not what I expected.	Told tutor and was able to transfer without losing any money.
Felt everyone in the class was cleverer than me – used to put off doing work or making presentations.	Talked it over with fellow students, found they felt the same. Developed a support group to discuss things we found hard.
Have always struggled with reading and writing, and this put me off, even though I was really interested in the course.	Joined the Study Support Unit and received one-to-one tuition (see Chapter 18).
There was a culture of not doing well amongst other students on the course, and many weren't at all motivated.	Decided I was going to ignore them – I had different reasons for being there and I was going to be very well motivated!
Too tired due to work and family commitments.	Decided to put off my studies until I had more time to concentrate.
Thought I needed to watch every soap opera on television.	Sold the television. Drastic, but worked.
Worried about failing.	Spoke to personal tutor who agreed to read drafts of my assignments before I handed them in. Found out that I had nothing at all to worry about and did very well on my course.

Table 3. Methods for dealing with poor motivation

However, when I conducted some research with adult learners it was found that some adults experienced profound dips in these levels of motivation. Often, this was not through their making, but was instead due to outside influences over which adults felt they had very little control. Table 3 lists these influences, along with suggestions, from adult learners, for coping with the situation.

Most people experience dips in their motivation levels at points during their lives. It is natural and nothing to be concerned about. However, where your studies are concerned, there are a few tips you can take note of to help keep your levels of motivation high:

◆ Make sure that you choose a subject in which you feel you have a high level of interest.

◆ Think about your learning style and try to choose a course and learning provider that will not clash with this style.

◆ Before you begin your course, write down your reasons for returning to learning. Keep the list in a prominent place and refer back to it when you feel your motivation levels dropping.

◆ Set yourself clear aims and objectives. What do you hope to achieve from the course? How do you intend to meet your goals?

◆ If you find that you are experiencing personal and family problems, don't ignore them as they may escalate. Tackle them as soon as they occur.

◆ Utilise available help at your college or university, such
as student support groups, counsellors and study support
(see Chapter 18).

PREPARING A STUDY PLAN

A study plan is a strategy you use to help you achieve the
most from your studies. It should help your studies to
become more efficient, effective and successful. Creating a
study plan is a very individual process – the guidelines listed
below will help at the start of your course, but as your
studies progress, you may find that you adapt your study
plan to suit your individual style and needs.

Setting your Goals

A goal is a clear statement that describes what you will be
able to do at the end of your studies. This will include
specific behaviour and a clear outcome. Most course information should contain a list of the 'course outcomes'. Read
these through and see if they match your own stated goals. If
there is a mismatch, you need to think about whether the
course is right for you.

Listing your Study Tasks

As you read the information about your course, you will
begin to form an idea of what actions or tasks you will be
required to undertake. Make a list of these tasks. This could
include tasks such as memorising information, learning facts,
reading books, analysing books, writing assignments, and so
on.

Listing Potential Study Problems

Go through your list of study tasks and note any that you think will create problems. You could mark them in order of difficulty. Include in this list any other problems you think you may have with your study, such as lack of interest or your family making demands on your time.

Rectifying Study Problems

Work through your list of study problems and decide what action you are going to take to rectify each problem. For some problems it is perfectly acceptable to decide that the situation will be rectified over time as your course progresses. For example, many students find that their powers of argument and persuasion improve as they complete more assignments. For some of the other problems you might find it enough to decide to read the rest of this book or to visit the Study Support Unit at your college or university. Keep your list of problems and refer back to it at the end of your course. You will be surprised how many of the difficulties were very easy to overcome or, in fact, were not problems at all.

Identifying your Strengths and Weaknesses

Some adults find it useful to identify their strengths and weaknesses before beginning their studies. Again, this helps you to work out what problems you might face on your course and think about coping strategies before the problems escalate. It is useful to think about your strengths as it helps you to feel positive about your ability to complete the course. You can also refer back to this list at the end of your course to see how your strengths and weaknesses have changed.

Developing a Semester/Term Plan

Using your course materials and other information supplied by your tutor, find out what tasks you will need to complete by the end of the semester or term. Enter any important dates onto a wall calendar so that you don't miss any deadlines (see Chapter 3). List everything you will need to have done, including any study tasks you will want to have developed and any study problems you intend to have improved upon. At the end of the semester, refer to your list to see whether you have completed everything you hoped, or whether there is still room for improvement.

Developing a Weekly Plan

For many courses you will need to be quite specific about the tasks you have to complete each week. Some people find it useful to complete a weekly plan every week, whereas others find that this is a waste of time. It might be useful to complete a weekly plan for the first four weeks until you get into a routine. However, it is important to make sure that you don't spend more time producing plans than you do on your studies. In your weekly plan you could include all your lectures and seminars, any background reading you hope to achieve and any other study tasks (see Chapter 3).

SUMMARY

This chapter has discussed the importance of careful preparation for study. This includes not only personal preparation, but also preparation of your working environment. Your studies are likely to be more successful if you are motivated to learn. Maintaining health, creating a good working environment and receiving support and encouragement from others will help you to remain motivated.

To get the most out of your studies it is important to prepare a study plan, identifying your goals, your strengths and weaknesses and your hopes and aspirations. By developing a study plan you will begin to organise your study time more effectively. Time management and personal organisational skills are an essential part of successful study and are discussed in more depth in the following chapter.

③

Organising your Study

As an adult, with many other things going on in your life, you may find it harder than other students to organise your life for study. Your family may be demanding your attention or you may have to hold down a job while you are studying. Household chores may seem to be never-ending and other people may be constantly interrupting your personal study time. However, there are several methods available for dealing with these types of problems. This chapter offers practical advice and guidance for managing your time effectively and organising yourself for study.

MANAGING YOUR TIME

For adult students managing time can be difficult, especially when family and work commitments make constant demands on what should be your personal study time. It may be the case that at some point during your studies you will need to be tough on your family. You will need to set ground rules about being disturbed, about being given enough quiet time to complete your work. Try not to feel guilty when this happens – remind yourself that your whole family will benefit from your studies.

Time management is all about taking control of your own time. You need to be able to make things happen in a way that will benefit you and your studies, and you need to stop other people controlling your time. This does not mean that you neglect family and work commitments. Instead, *you* decide when you will spend time with your children, on your work, in social or recreational activities and on your studies.

The following points should help you to take control of your time:

◆ Draw up a list or create a chart of non-negotiable activities, in relation to your course and your home life, that you must carry out each week. This will include attending lectures, seminars and tutorials, and any other essential activities such as collecting children from school. Make sure that your family or employer knows that these cannot be altered and that you are unavailable at these times.

◆ Set aside some time for private study. If family commitments allow you, try to do this at a time that suits the way you like to study. Some people find that they are more creative and motivated in the mornings, whereas others find that they can work better in the evenings. If you're not sure which you prefer, try working at different times of the day for the first few weeks to see if you have a preference. If you don't have the luxury of choosing your study time, still set aside blocks within the time you have available and make sure that everyone knows that you are not to be disturbed.

◆ You should avoid marathon study sessions – shorter sessions tend to be more productive, especially in terms of committing material to memory.

◆ Don't work at a time when you should be sleeping – sleep is essential for your intellectual, emotional and physical health.

◆ If possible, set a clear start and stopping time for your study sessions. You will find that you begin to read faster, but do not lose any understanding of the material (see Chapter 4).

◆ Drop any worthless or pointless activities. You may not have many of these, but think about what you do during the day and consider whether there is anything you do that is wasting your time.

◆ Think of the most efficient way to carry out a task or cope with a problem. Many student hours are wasted trying to sort out a computer problem or to find a particular reference in the library. Rather than struggle on and waste time, ask someone instead. Contact the computer help desk, ask a knowledgeable friend or speak to a librarian. Never be afraid to ask, especially when it saves your valuable time.

◆ Recreation and socialising are important for your frame of mind and well-being. Make sure that you keep enough time spare each week for these activities, although you should make sure that you strike the right balance between these activities and your studies. Remember that work and play don't mix – when you are relaxing don't think about work, and when you are working, don't think about what you will be doing on Saturday night.

Students over the age of eighteen were asked what they considered to be their worst time-wasting activities. These are listed in the box below, and will help you to think about your own time wasting activities as your studies progress.

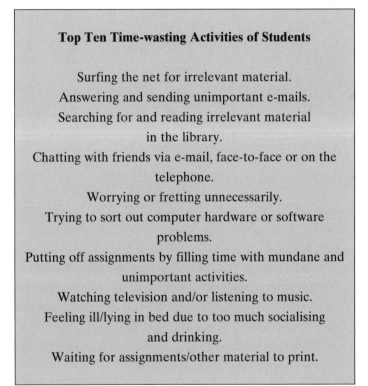

Top Ten Time-wasting Activities of Students

Surfing the net for irrelevant material.
Answering and sending unimportant e-mails.
Searching for and reading irrelevant material
in the library.
Chatting with friends via e-mail, face-to-face or on the
telephone.
Worrying or fretting unnecessarily.
Trying to sort out computer hardware or software
problems.
Putting off assignments by filling time with mundane and
unimportant activities.
Watching television and/or listening to music.
Feeling ill/lying in bed due to too much socialising
and drinking.
Waiting for assignments/other material to print.

COMPLETING COURSEWORK AND MEETING DEADLINES

An important part of time management when you are study-ing is making sure that you complete your work on time and meet all the deadlines you have been given. All assignments should be handed in on time. Some institutions are very strict about this and, unless you have a very good reason for missing a deadline, your work will be unmarked and may affect your final result.

The following points will help you to think about meeting deadlines and handing in your work on time:

◆ At the beginning of your course you should be given a timetable that includes all the assignment and project deadlines. Using a wall calendar (these can be obtained from Students' Union shops) mark all assignment and project deadlines in red. Display your chart in a prominent place and refer to it often so that you become familiar with specific deadlines.

◆ Complete all assignments at least three days before the deadline. That way you should not be held up by unforeseen problems such as printer queues, computer crashes or family crises.

◆ Do not procrastinate. The definition of 'procrastinate' is 'to defer, to delay from day to day'. Don't put off your work. When you need to complete a piece of work for your course, start as soon as possible. Don't find other things to do with your time, especially things that can wait or can be done by someone else.

◆ If you find that you really are having problems completing your work, stop and do something else for a while. You will find it easier to approach your work if you are refreshed. If you start each assignment early enough, you will have plenty of time to do this.

◆ Talk over problems with fellow students or your tutor. Often you will find another mind helps you to overcome your block.

◆ Hand in assignments on time, even if they are not perfect or complete. You will still get some marks and maybe they are not as bad as you think.

KEEPING A LEARNING DIARY

Many adult students find it useful to keep a learning diary. Indeed, on some courses you will be asked to complete a learning diary as part of your coursework because it is useful to your learning. If you think about what you are doing on your course and regularly analyse what you are learning by writing a diary, you will find that you begin to understand better the content of your course. This will help you to remember and recall the information more easily at a later date.

Your learning diary can also be a record of how you feel on the course – the problems you are facing, the excitement of learning new things, the relationships you are developing with fellow students and with the tutors. It can be a useful exercise to write down your anxieties, fears and concerns because this will help you to work through them. It is also very helpful to record all the high points because it will serve as a reminder of why you have enrolled on the course.

Some students find it useful to record their aims and objectives, or to set their goals, within a learning diary. They find it useful to return to the diary throughout the course to see whether they are meeting their aims and objectives and to determine whether the course is meeting their needs. Others prefer to keep a record of everything they have learned.

The language within your learning diary should be kept plain and simple, and valuable and constructive comments should be made, rather than simple comments such as 'it was good'.

Learning diaries can be very personal and you may not wish to share your diary with anyone else. The way that you make entries in your diary, what you decide to include and what you do with the diary at the end of the course is totally up to you. In the box below are listed various questions that you may wish to answer within your learning diary.

Learning Diary – Questions

What are your short- and long-term goals?

What steps do you need to take to achieve these goals?

What do you hope to achieve by attending the course?

What progress have you made on the course?

What work has not gone well? Why do you think you have struggled? What can you do to improve the situation?

What do you think about the content of the course? How has it helped you?

What have you learned on the course?

Do you agree with everything you have been taught or are there points with which you disagree?

Is there anything you don't understand on which you need to spend extra time?

How does the course relate to your previous knowledge and experience?

Is there anything you can offer other students and the tutor in relation to your knowledge and experience?

Have your attitudes and beliefs changed as a result of attending the course? If so, in what way?

Has attending the course changed your plans for the future?

Will these plans involve further learning and, if so, what do you need to do to continue your learning?

OVERCOMING DIFFICULTIES WITH PERSONAL ORGANISATION

During some research with adult learners I found that one of the main barriers to further learning was that people felt there was not enough time available to study. However, they pointed out that if their motivation levels were high enough, they were able to find this time, even though they thought it had been unavailable previously.

The students were asked how this time had been freed and their answers provide useful tips for other adults in similar positions.

Anne (39)

I really thought I had no time at all. I had to take the kids to school, pick them up, wash and iron their clothes, sort out my husband and his lunch and everything, walk the dog. The list was endless. But then I realised I was just making excuses. I enrolled on a course and I decided my husband could make his own lunch – it was no big deal. I even got him to do tea for the kids every now and again. I walked the dog when I took and fetched the kids and I did the washing only twice a week. The course fitted around school hours and then I told everyone I had to have some study time at weekends – three hours Saturday morning and three hours Sunday morning. I got up early while they were all still in bed. They thought it was a treat because they were allowed to play in their rooms without me nagging them to get dressed. In the end I realised no one was suffering at all. And I passed my course!

Ned (45)

Five years I used to say I'd got no time. Then I were threatened with redundancy and all of a sudden I thought, yes, I've got the time, even though I were doing exactly the same stuff. I think the hardest thing were going to evening classes in winter, though, oh it were cold. But I decided to buy a computer and the next course were online. It meant I didn't have to go out. I worked from home in the evenings and at weekends. I made sure I had a comfortable room, nice desk and chair, that's right important, that. I'd put answer machine on and not answer door. Then I could concentrate on what I were doing. I'd plenty of time as long as I sat down and just did it, you know, didn't get distracted with washing-up and stuff like that.

Martha (58)

Bill just wouldn't leave me alone when I was working, where's this and where's that? I wouldn't be able to get anything done and then the day would be over. It was like having a two-year-old in the house. He's retired and it was driving me potty. I decided while he was in the house I would be out of the house. I did all my work in the college library. It helped being with other students who all wanted to work. Bill could potter about at home to his heart's content. Then we would spend the evening together and not get on each other's nerves. I do all my work in the library now and they have computers which makes my life easier.

SUMMARY

This chapter has discussed the importance of organising your study. As an adult you will have considerable demands on your time, but for study to be successful you need to try to reduce these demands and create an environment conducive to learning. To do this you need to develop and enhance your skills of time management and personal organisation.

Many students find that their personal organisation skills develop as their studies progress. One way this happens is that, with practice, your studies become more efficient. The next chapter offers advice on enhancing your reading skills so that your reading becomes more effective, efficient and successful.

4

Enhancing your
Reading Skills

Reading is not solely about reading the words on the page. There are many different aspects to the reading process, as illustrated in the box below. To be successful in your studies, you will need to enhance your reading skills so that you can tackle the different types of reading required on your course. This chapter offers advice on how to do this.

PREPARING FOR ACADEMIC READING

To be able to read academic texts you will need to have well developed linguistic, visual and auditory skills. Most adults have developed their linguistic skills over a lifetime and will not need to have these checked out. However, if you have not had your eyes tested for some time it is advisable to do so as undiagnosed poor eyesight can have considerable negative influence on your reading ability. Also, it may be advisable to have your hearing tested as this can affect your listening skills and note-taking ability which in turn will have an influence on how you read and revise your notes.

When you begin to prepare yourself for academic reading, it

is useful to be aware of the different aspects of the reading process. These are listed in the box below.

Aspects of the Reading Process

Recognising letter sounds and the sounds of words

Recognising the meaning of words

Understanding the sequence in which the words have been written

Recognising the look of words

Predicting the order of the words

Predicting the ideas contained within the words

Skimming to get a general idea of what the text is about

Skimming to recap what has been said

Scanning to search for information to help predict

Scanning to disregard irrelevant material

Scanning for key words

Understanding the meaning of the text

Looking for meaning outside the context of the sentence

Analysing what has been said and what has not been said

Critiquing what you have read

USING READING LISTS

On most courses you will be presented with a reading list. Do not rush out and buy all the books on the list as it can be expensive and in most cases is not necessary. Ask your tutor which are the key texts and which will be the most useful on your course, then make a decision about what you want to buy.

If your tutor has given you a long reading list, don't be daunted by the number of books. Some tutors will include a greater number than necessary because they realise that students may have difficulty getting hold of books in the library, or the list offers a wider variety of themes and ideas.

Use reading lists carefully. Ask your tutor which are the important books. Find out if your tutor has a suggestion for starting your reading – are some of the books easier to read than others? Should some be left until later, when you have begun to understand some of the ideas and concepts?

If you have difficulty getting hold of any of the books, speak to your tutor. They will be able to recommend alternatives or offer suggestions about where a copy might be obtained. You can also use the bibliography of relevant books to find other books that may be of use.

DEVELOPING YOUR ACADEMIC READING

For successful reading to take place the reading matter needs to be appropriate, relevant and suited to your individual style and interests. As an adult you have enrolled on a course in which you are interested, so this will help you to read and understand books relevant to your course. However, if you have no experience of a particular course, or of a particular academic style of writing, you may find it harder to understand what you are reading.

This is a problem faced by many students – reading complex academic texts is a new experience that can be daunting. What you should remember is that for successful reading to take place practice is essential, and with adequate practice you will soon understand what you are reading.

As a student you will not only be reading for meaning and accuracy, but you will also be reading for thought. What you read will help you to develop your own ideas about the subject. This means that the reading process also involves your own personality, experiences and imagination. Reading is not passive but is an active process in which you draw from your own experiences, develop your own thoughts and learn to evaluate and critique the thoughts and ideas presented within the text.

You can develop your academic reading skills by considering the following points:

◆ Do not put off your reading. Begin as soon as you start the course, if not before.

◆ Do not ignore books aimed at someone younger or at the lay person – they might help to explain something with which you are struggling. You can move on to more complex texts once you have grasped the general idea.

◆ Learn how to use contents pages and indexes carefully. You will not have time to read every book from cover to cover, and on most courses this is not necessary. Think about the key issues or topics needed for your course or assignment and read sections of books that are relevant to these issues.

◆ Before you begin your reading, write down what information you want and the questions you wish to answer.

This will help you to focus your reading and stop you becoming distracted on irrelevant material. When you've finished reading a section, see if there are any questions that remain unanswered.

◆ Read introductions and summaries to find out whether the book or chapter is relevant. If it is not relevant, discard it for something else.

◆ Try to *understand* and *evaluate* what you are reading. Do not read page after page without understanding the material. If you don't understand a text, discuss it with other students or with your tutor, or try another text which might explain the concepts in a better way. There are additional techniques you can use when faced with complex data and figures (see Chapter 6).

◆ Take notes as you read.

◆ Set manageable sections for your reading. With time you will begin to understand your own concentration levels. Work within these levels – if you read for too long you will find that you are unable to retain much of your reading or take in new information. Always have short breaks within your reading sessions to refresh your mind.

◆ Always keep your purpose in mind when reading.

IMPROVING YOUR READING SPEED

On some courses you may appear to have so much reading to complete that you feel completely overwhelmed. However, you should not let these feelings put you off your reading. You will be surprised how much reading you can complete on your course, especially if you consider the points outlined below:

◆ Reading speed improves with practice. The more you practise the faster you will read.

◆ Reading speed improves with comprehension. As you become more familiar with your subject and the technical jargon used, you will find that you read faster. You will spend less time reviewing what you have read in an effort to understand the material.

◆ Reading speed improves with interest. If you are interested in what you are reading you will find that you read faster, especially when you are intrigued to know what happens next.

◆ Reading speed improves with motivation. If your motivation levels remain high you will find it easier to read at a quicker pace and take in the material.

There are several reasons why people read slowly. It is not advisable to force yourself to read more quickly without addressing these reasons as you may simply begin to read more quickly but not improve your understanding of the material. Table 4 below outlines possible reasons for slow reading. The second column gives suggestions for solving the problem and hence improving reading speed without losing comprehension.

Although it is desirable to increase your reading speed, to be successful in your studies you will need to know when to adjust your rate. You will encounter some situations when it

REASON FOR SLOW READING	METHOD FOR IMPROVING SPEED
The need to read the material word-by-word.	Try to concentrate on key words and meaningful ideas rather than sounding out each word. Try to develop a wider eye-span which will help you to read more than one word at a time. This aids comprehension.
Being slow to recognise and respond to material, usually due to technical jargon or difficult concepts and ideas.	This will improve as you become more familiar with your subject. Talk through difficult ideas with other students or your tutor, or read another book that is easier to understand. If one sentence or paragraph is slowing you down, move on – it could become clearer as you read more.
The need to read the material out loud.	Learn to read silently. Concentrate on the ideas presented rather than individual words.
Problems with eyesight.	Have your eyesight checked. Often slow reading is due to poor eyesight which has not been corrected.
Problems with eye movements.	Faulty eye movements can lead to problems with finding your place on the page which will slow down your reading. A visit to your optician could solve the problem.
Lack of concentration.	Read at a time when you are most productive, not when you are tired. Break reading sessions down into small, manageable chunks.

Table 4. Improving reading speed

Distractions.	Find a quiet place to read, free from distractions. Notice when you distract yourself from reading, and learn how to pull your mind back to the task.
Lack of practice.	Practise as much as possible. Many students find that this is the most effective way to improve reading speeds.
Habitual slow reading.	If you have always read slowly it can be difficult to change, but it is possible. Begin by taking a simple text and force yourself to read more quickly, without losing meaning. Gradually practise with more complex texts. Be aware of your reading rate and notice when you revert to slower reading.
Re-reading the material.	If you read slowly you may find you have to re-read material to take it in. However, try not to do this – most ideas will be repeated again in the text. As your reading speed improves you will find less need to re-read.
Trying to remember everything.	Consider what is important and remember facts selectively. This could be helped by writing a list of important issues prior to beginning reading.
Dyslexia.	If you have been diagnosed with dyslexia, or you think you might be dyslexic, find out what support is offered by your learning provider (see Chapter 18).

is important to slow down your reading, as the following list illustrates:

◆ Unfamiliar terminology that needs exploring.

◆ Difficult sentence or paragraph construction that needs unpicking.

◆ Detailed technical instruction that needs clear understanding.

◆ Unfamiliar or abstract concepts that need extra attention.

◆ Ideas that need retaining.

On the other hand you can rapidly increase the speed of your reading when you encounter the following:

◆ Material with which you are familiar and are being told nothing new.

◆ Irrelevant case studies, examples, illustrations or tables.

◆ Too much detail or elaboration that is unnecessary to your purpose.

◆ Broad generalisations of ideas that have been previously stated.

TAKING NOTES FROM BOOKS

Taking notes from books is a personal process and as your course progresses you will find a method that best suits you. However, there are a few points you should note from the start of your reading as this will make it easier to review your notes and prepare for examinations and essay writing:

◆ Make notes which will aid your understanding and help you to review and revise what you have read.

◆ Do not copy chunks of text from the book. Read the relevant sections, think about what you have read and make a few brief notes written in your own words. This will help you to make sure that you are not using the sentences of others in your written work.

◆ If you come across a useful quotation, write it down exactly, word-for word. Check that you have copied it correctly if you intend to use it in an assignment. In your notes, write 'quotation' in the margin, or use quotation marks so that you are clear it is a quotation. Make sure that you note the page number, the author of the book, the title of the book and the place and date of publication. It can be time-consuming and frustrating trying to locate quotations that you wish to use at a later date.

◆ Organise your notes. File your notes with other notes on the same topic. This will make it easier to find the relevant information when you need to revise or write an essay. Some students find it useful to write the main ideas onto cards and file them in a card index.

SUMMARY

This chapter has discussed the development of reading skills. There are several different aspects to the reading process and as an adult student you will need to develop these skills to get the most out of your reading. Through practice you will find that your reading speed increases without loss of comprehension, and increasingly you will be able to understand more complex academic texts.

As your reading improves you will find that your writing skills also improve. With practice, you will become more efficient at taking notes and your reading will become more effective and enjoyable. The next chapter offers advice on enhancing your writing skills which will in turn aid your reading skills.

5

Enhancing your Writing Skills

English sentences are shaped by various rules and conventions; for example, they start with a capital letter and end with a full stop. As an adult you will have learned many of these rules and conventions over your lifetime. You might think that your punctuation, grammar, spelling and vocabulary are not very good, but you have a great deal of existing knowledge and experience on which you can draw to make the small improvements needed to pass your assignments. This chapter offers advice and guidance on making these small improvements.

If you are really concerned about your ability to write well enough, think about seeking extra help from a Study Support Unit (see Chapter 18). However, most adults find that any problems they face are more to do with a lack of confidence in their own ability, and once they have practised writing and received positive feedback, the process becomes a lot easier.

IMPROVING PUNCTUATION AND GRAMMAR

Punctuation is used to help the writer to get their message

across in a clear and concise manner. When we speak we make the meaning clear by pausing, expressing words in different ways and adding facial and hand gestures. We cannot do this in writing, so instead we use punctuation to give our sentences a clear meaning.

If you find that concentrating on your punctuation and grammar distracts you from what you are writing, try writing down all your ideas first without thinking too much about the punctuation and grammar. Once your ideas are written on paper, you can go over your work and add commas and semi-colons, check tenses and so on. Although many tutors require you to construct your sentences and punctuate properly, they are most interested in the ideas and arguments that you express in your work.

For your first few assignments you might find it useful to have your work checked over by a fellow student who can point out any problems before you hand in the assignment. Some tutors might be willing to look over a draft assignment if they have time, but check first whether this is the case.

It is not possible to discuss all aspects of punctuation and grammar within this book. However, the following points help to address the most common problems faced by adult students.

Capital Letters

There are seven rules to follow when using capital letters:

◆ You *always* start a sentence with a capital letter.

◆ The pronoun 'I' is always written as a capital letter.

◆ Proper nouns, such as names of people and names of places, begin with a capital letter.

◆ Capital letters are used to begin the first word and the other main words in the title of a book, e.g. *Learning How to Study Again.*

◆ When you are referring to a particular month or a particular day of the week you use a capital letter.

◆ Capital letters are used at the beginning of a passage of direct speech, even if it is not the beginning of a sentence, e.g. *she said, 'When will he arrive?'*

◆ Capital letters are used in abbreviations only if capital letters are used for the full word or title, e.g. The Royal Society for the Prevention of Cruelty to Animals – RSPCA.

The Comma

Commas indicate the shortest pause in a sentence. They can be used in six different ways:

◆ To divide the items in a list, although a comma is not used to divide the last two words if they are separated by 'and', e.g. *carpets, curtains, lampshades and furniture.*

◆ To separate two or more adjectives connected to a noun, e.g. *she was a shy, modest woman.*

◆ If you want to insert an extra phrase into a sentence, you separate it from the main sentence by using commas. To check that you have put the commas in the right place, read the sentence without the inserted phrase and see if it still makes sense, e.g. *focus groups, although criticised by some people, are a useful method of data collection.*

◆ If you use the adverbs *however, therefore* or *nevertheless* in mid-sentence, you would separate these by commas, e.g. *focus groups, therefore, were the best method to use in this research.*

◆ If you wish to add a phrase on to your main sentence you would use a comma to separate the phrase, e.g. *she decided to use focus groups in her research, even though she had no experience of the data collection technique.*

◆ Direct speech is preceded by a comma, e.g. *she said, 'I will enjoy using focus groups.'*

The Semi-Colon

The semi-colon indicates a pause slightly longer than a comma. It is used in three ways:

◆ The semi-colon should be used when dividing the items of a list when additional information about each item is supplied, e.g. *carpets, which were red; curtains that had faded in the light; lampshades too numerous to mention and various items of furniture.*

◆ Semi-colons can be used to join two closely connected sentences, e.g. *the focus group ran smoothly; she had been a good facilitator.*

◆ Semi-colons can be used in front of an adverb to indicate a slightly longer pause than a comma, e.g. *the focus group finished after two hours of intensive discussion; so she was happy and went home.*

The Colon

The colon indicates a slightly longer pause than the semi-colon but a slightly shorter pause than a full stop. Colons are used for two purposes:

◆ To indicate the start of a list.

◆ To indicate the start of a long quotation.

Brackets

Brackets are useful punctuation marks for students. They are used in three main ways:

◆ To reference a piece of material in your written text, e.g. *(Dawson, 2003:34).*

◆ To add an extra piece of information to your sentence, e.g. *the course fees are £2,300 (inclusive of field trips and materials).*

◆ To add information after a person's name e.g. *Thomas Hardy (author).*

The Apostrophe

Apostrophes are one of the punctuation marks that students often get wrong. The most common mistake is that they are used when they are not needed. In fact, they are used only in two ways:

◆ To show where a letter has been missed out, e.g. *it's (it is), don't (do not) and can't (cannot).*

◆ To show ownership, e.g. *my mother's books (the books of my mother).* In this example the books belong to one person so the apostrophe is written before the 's'. However, if the books belong to several people, the apostrophe appears after the 's' to denote ownership, e.g. *our mothers' books (the books of our mothers).*

The Dash

The dash is used to lengthen the pause between words and can be used in two main ways:

◆ It can be used instead of commas or brackets when you want to insert extra information into a sentence, e.g. *the focus group was attended by eight people – three men and five women – and was a complete success.*

◆ You can use it in the middle of a sentence when you wish to change the thought or idea being expressed, but don't want a full stop, e.g. *I found essays really hard going – but that has improved now.*

The Hyphen

A hyphen is used to shorten the pause between words. It can be used in four main ways:

◆ To link two or more words together to form a word that has a different meaning, e.g. *daughter-in-law, well-known.*

◆ To link prefixes, e.g. *pre-war, ex-champion.*

◆ To show that vowels are pronounced separately, e.g. *co-operative.*

◆ To make the meaning of a sentence clearer, e.g. *we expect you to attend for two hour-long lectures.*

IMPROVING SPELLING

Spelling is a skill you learn by reading and writing. If you do not read and write regularly your spelling will not improve. Also spelling is a visual skill – with the experience that you have gained over your lifetime, you will find that you have learned to recognise when words look right. You will find that with practice this skill continues with academic words or technical jargon with which you are presently unfamiliar. When you come to proofread your work, you will find that you notice when words look wrong.

English words can be very hard to spell because many of them do not follow a regular pattern. If you think your spelling is bad, you are not alone. The first thing you need to do is to get hold of a good dictionary and then use it – it will help you with the spelling, the meaning and the proper use of the word. The more you use a dictionary, the more your spelling will improve. Don't rely completely on the spell-check facility on your computer – it will pick up some words that have been spelt incorrectly, but it will miss many others and it won't aid your comprehension of the word.

The following tips address the areas with which adult learners tend to struggle. However, these are general rules and there are always exceptions. If in doubt about any spelling, consult your dictionary.

◆ Perhaps the most famous rule is '*put i before e, except after c.*' The exceptions to this rule include words such as *forfeit, weird, neighbour* and *either.*

◆ For many short words you double the last letter when you add an ending to them, e.g. *omitted, fatter, biggest, dropping.* Exceptions to this rule include *buses, gases* and *entering.*

◆ If a word ends with a silent 'e', when you are adding anything to the word you drop the 'e', e.g. *caring, shining, conceivable.* However, you keep the 'e' when there is a soft-sounding 'ce' or 'ge' ending, e.g. *changeable, noticeable.*

◆ Short words that end in 'll' only have one 'l' when you add to the word, e.g. *handful, welcome, until.* Exceptions to this rule include *farewell, illness* and *tallness.*

◆ Adjectives with one 'l' usually take a double 'll' when they become adverbs, e.g. *real/really, careful/carefully.*

◆ Verbs ending in 'ie' drop the 'e' when adding 'ing' or 'ed', e.g. *lie/lying/lied.* Notice also that the 'i' changes to a 'y' because you can't have a double 'ii'.

◆ If a word ends in a double consonant and you add an ending, it is usual to retain both consonants, e.g. *assess/ assessment.*

◆ When you add 'ness' to a word that ends in 'n' it is usual to keep a double 'nn' e.g. *keen/keenness.*

◆ When a word ends in 'oe' you keep the letter 'e' when adding to the word, e.g. *hoe/hoeing*. However, if your addition begins with 'e' you will drop the 'e', e.g. *hoe/hoed*.

◆ When adding an extra part to a word, both consonants are retained so you have a double consonant within the words, e.g. *unnecessary (un + necessary), withhold (with + hold)*.

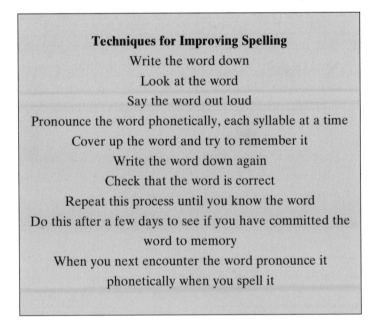

Techniques for Improving Spelling
Write the word down
Look at the word
Say the word out loud
Pronounce the word phonetically, each syllable at a time
Cover up the word and try to remember it
Write the word down again
Check that the word is correct
Repeat this process until you know the word
Do this after a few days to see if you have committed the word to memory
When you next encounter the word pronounce it phonetically when you spell it

IMPROVING VOCABULARY

As your course progresses, you will find that your vocabulary will increase as you read, write and use your dictionary. However, you can help to increase your vocabulary further by considering the following points:

◆ When you encounter a new word in your lectures or seminars, write it down and look it up after your lecture has finished. You might find it useful to keep a separate notebook that contains definitions of new words.

◆ Don't skip over or ignore words that you don't understand.

◆ If you encounter new words during your reading, make a note of the word and use your dictionary or the 'glossary of terms' to find its meaning. If the word is crucial to understand the meaning of what you are reading, you will need to do this immediately. However, it is usually better not to disrupt your reading, but to look up all the words that you don't understand when you have finished.

◆ Don't be afraid to ask tutors what something means – other students probably don't know what it means but don't want to ask – they will be pleased that you have had the courage to do so.

◆ Read as much as you can.

◆ Try to use any new words that you have learned in your speech or writing to reinforce their meaning.

WRITING AT THE CORRECT LEVEL AND PITCH

Many adult learners who are new to writing assignments worry that they are not pitching their work at the correct level. Obviously, this will depend upon your course – someone studying for a degree will have to pitch their assignment at a more complex level than someone studying for a GCSE, for example.

The best way to overcome this problem is to ask your tutor to provide examples of successful assignments completed by previous students on the course. Read through the assignments and ask yourself the following questions:

1) How has the assignment been written?
2) What information has been included?
3) How has the author structured their argument?
4) What technical jargon has been used?
5) How much knowledge of the subject does the reader require to be able to understand the writing?
6) Do *you* understand what has been written?

If you are still finding it difficult to understand what is required, speak to your tutor. Ask them to work through the above questions on a couple of assignments. They might be able to provide you with an example of an essay that has not been pitched at the correct level – by reading through this essay you will be able to avoid mistakes in your own assignments.

Some tutors may prefer not to provide examples of other work because they believe that this may stifle your creativeness. If this is the case, write a draft assignment and discuss it thoroughly with your tutor, who will be able to give you positive and constructive feedback for your final version. Take note of all feedback provided by your tutors. Learn from your mistakes and produce a better assignment next time. If you don't understand the feedback, or where you have gone wrong, ask your tutor for clarification.

SUMMARY

This chapter has provided advice and guidance on enhancing your academic writing skills. Many adults are concerned about their ability to write well. However, you will find that, with practice, your writing skills will improve considerably. Through small improvements in punctuation, grammar, vocabulary and spelling, you will find that you are able to produce better-written projects and assignments. Further advice for producing successful assignments is provided in Chapter 11.

The next chapter looks at ways in which you can enhance your mathematical and scientific skills.

6

Enhancing your Mathematical and Scientific Skills

If you feel worried about your mathematical skills you are not alone – feelings of insecurity about mathematics are widespread in the adult population. Many adults feel anxious, helpless and worried when they are confronted with a mathematical problem. In many cases adults complain that their brains have 'gone dead' and they are unable to think about the problem without breaking out in a cold sweat. Even the most highly-educated people can turn to jelly when asked to sort out a mathematical equation or work out a fraction or percentage.

Yet maths and science should be viewed as being no more complex than any of the other subjects we have learned over our lives. With a little perseverance, and perhaps with the help of a good, patient tutor, adults find that they are able to grasp and understand what they initially thought were complex mathematical and scientific concepts.

Although advice and guidance for improving your mathematical and scientific skills is offered in this chapter it is not possible to cover basic maths in this book. If you have to complete a maths component on your course, and you feel that you are really struggling, find out what support is available from the Study Support Unit at your college or university (see Chapter 18).

READING MATHEMATICAL AND SCIENTIFIC MATERIAL

Mathematics and science courses might need less reading than that required for other subjects, but they do require you to understand and master the concepts about which you are reading. Writers of scientific material often pack together a large amount of facts and figures and students tend to feel compelled to wade through the text in a logical, sequential order.

However, scientific and mathematical texts contain clues about what is being presented – headings, subheadings, summaries, conclusions. You will find it more effective to skim and scan the material, spending extra time on the relevant sections and moving quickly through the less relevant information. By doing this you will be able to cover a greater number of texts and your comprehension of what is being discussed will also improve.

You can help to enhance the effectiveness of reading scientific and mathematical material by considering the following points:

◆ When faced with a scientific or mathematical text skim through the material to get an overview of the ideas presented. Pay particular attention to the introduction, summary and conclusion.

◆ Try to build up an overview of the information first by scanning the relevant sections and trying to work out how they all fit together. Look for key words or phrases that help you to understand and piece together what you are reading. In this way you will not be trying to memorise hundreds of isolated facts but will be able to understand the bigger picture.

◆ When you skim and scan a text, be aware of words or terms that are new to you. See if you can find a definition within the text, but if not, refer to a glossary or dictionary. Keep a record of the term and definition, including a page reference, as this will help you when it comes to revising.

◆ Try to *understand* what you are reading rather than memorising the facts. You will probably need to memorise some information, but you will find this easier to do if you understand what you are trying to remember.

◆ Try covering up some of the material you are reading and work through the ideas or figures in your head. You will get a feel for your level of understanding.

◆ Pay particular attention to charts and figures. Scientific texts usually summarise major ideas and facts in graphic form.

UNDERSTANDING CHARTS, TABLES AND GRAPHS

Some people find that their minds go blank when they are faced with what appear to be complex tables, charts and graphs. However, if you work your way logically through the figures, you will soon find that you begin to understand what you are seeing. The following tips should help you to do this:

◆ Look first at the main headings. Do they give you an idea of what the table is about?

◆ Look at the headings in each column or the titles on the axes. Are you clear about what is included in each of these columns?

◆ Pick a figure inserted into one part of the table or on the graph. Try to work out what the figure is telling you.

◆ Scan the table or graph for interesting figures or anomalies.

◆ Can you see any particular trends? What do they mean?

◆ What are the high and low points? Why might this be?

◆ Are there any blips or unusual figures? What do they show? Why might this have occurred?

◆ Try turning the numbers into words.

◆ Summarise the main conclusions that you can draw from the chart.

◆ Write down any ideas that you have as this will help you to move your thinking from abstract numbers to written material.

PRODUCING CHARTS, TABLES AND GRAPHS ON A COMPUTER

There are a number of different computer programs that can be used to produce graphs, charts and tables:

◆ Spreadsheets

◆ Word processors

◆ Presentation graphics packages

◆ Desktop publishers

◆ Specialist programs.

In most cases, the easier a program is to use, the less sophisticated will be the presentation of the graphs, charts and tables. However, unless you are studying on a course that requires complex presentation of statistical data, you should find that some of the simpler programs are perfectly adequate for your requirements.

As you will see in Chapter 10, the majority of students use Microsoft software and products. The following steps are based on this type of software. If your college or university uses other software, seek advice and guidance from your Computing Services Department. In general you will need to follow the steps outlined below to produce your graphs, charts and tables:

◆ **Step 1 – Indicate that you wish to make a table**. Look for the relevant button in one of your menus (this could be the *edit*, *insert* or *table* button). At this stage you may get the chance to say what type of table or chart you require. You can choose a ready-made chart or design one of your own.

◆ **Step 2 – Edit your table**. In most cases you will need to type your titles and numbers into the table or change the titles and numbers that have automatically appeared. Click on one of the boxes (cells) in the table and type in your word or number. If there is something in the cell already, your number or word will replace it. Press *enter* and click on other cells to alter the rest of the table.

◆ **Step 3 – Change the look of your table**. You can do this by viewing the options available in the *format* menu. You may need to highlight your table first, or you can just click on each option to see what your table would look like in different formats, including the various types of graphs. You will also find options for changing the chart type, axes and colours.

◆ **Step 4 – Save your work**. Think of a suitable name and location in which to save your chart. It may seem obvious, but some students forget to do this and then find it impossible to retrieve their work.

◆ **Step 5 – Print your work**. If you are given a choice of printers you need to be aware that a draft printer at your college may not print graphs. For a high-quality copy you will need to use a good quality printer. You may find that you need to edit your chart, table or graph – for example, with different colours or shading – to get clearer distinctions between the different parts.

COPING WITH PROBLEM SHEETS

For most mathematics and science courses you will be required to complete problem sheets. Again, this is nothing to be worried about – with a little preparation and careful analysis you will find that you are able to work your way through the problems presented. The following tips should help you to do this:

◆ Begin working on problem sheets as soon as possible. If they are not assessed, don't wait for the answers as this will not help you to understand the topic. Exam questions may include many of the issues covered on these sheets, so if you understand what you are learning you will do better in your exams.

◆ Always work through problem sheets before the seminar is held on the topic. It will make more sense to you when the issues are discussed and you can ask questions on issues you have not been able to understand. Don't be afraid to do this as the seminar leader will be pleased for the contribution.

◆ Make sure you understand thoroughly what you are being asked to do – if not, clarify with your tutor.

◆ Many problems can be solved through the use of a good diagram or model. This will help you to simplify and interpret the problem.

◆ Write down what you are doing. This helps you to keep a note of the procedures you have used and helps you to retrace your steps if things go wrong. It will also help you to better understand abstract concepts.

- ◆ If you are presented with multiple choice questions, make sure that you read all the options before you decide upon your answer.

- ◆ Try brainstorming with other students to help you work through difficult questions.

- ◆ Remember that even if you do not get the question right, you have learned a lot just by trying to solve the problem, so don't be disheartened.

CONDUCTING EXPERIMENTS

On many science courses you will be required to conduct experiments. Most adults find this an exciting prospect – indeed, this is probably one of the reasons why you have chosen to study a science subject. The procedures you use for your experiments will vary and depend upon the subject and level of your course, the requirements of your tutor and the equipment available to you. For degree-level courses you may be required to do the following:

- ◆ Think about a title for your work. Your title should describe in a clear, concise way the nature of your experiment. It should be meaningful and easily understood.

- ◆ Write a statement of your purpose. This should be short and succinct, describing clearly what you intend to do in your experiment. This will help you to focus your thoughts.

- ◆ Think about your methods. How do you intend to conduct your experiment? What are the different stages?

◆ Gather information about your topic. This may require a literature search, a review of lecture notes or discussion with tutors and other students.

◆ Identify and summarise significant points from the literature or from your discussions.

◆ Form a hypothesis. This is a statement about a phenomenon or observation that is put forward for testing (see Chapter 13).

◆ Decide what experiments are needed to test your hypothesis.

◆ Design your experiments. When you do this you may need to consider the following points:
   ◆ What materials do you require?
   ◆ From where will you obtain the materials?
   ◆ What are the health and safety considerations? Remember that this includes personal safety and the safety of others around you.

◆ Conduct your experiments. This may involve the following, depending upon the type of experiment:
   ◆ Changing one variable in each experiment.
   ◆ Accurate recording and measurement of results.
   ◆ Repetition of tests to verify findings.

◆ Summarise results and draw conclusions.

◆ Write up your results.

When you are conducting experiments you need to be aware that not all of them will be successful or produce the results you intended. This does not mean that you have failed – you can still learn from unsuccessful experiments. Unexpected results help you to modify and build upon your hypothesis until you are able to produce more successful results.

Avoiding Mistakes during Experiments

Some students assume that their hypothesis is right when they have not tested it thoroughly enough. This may be because it appears to be 'common sense' or 'obvious'. Don't get caught out in this way – all hypotheses should be tested thoroughly.

We are all human beings – sometimes we let our humanness get in the way of objectivity. This may be for many reasons – desire to succeed, lack of confidence, stubbornness, etc. Make sure that your emotions do not influence your experiments in an adverse way.

Some students do not spot important errors – be vigilant and make sure that you keep accurate records of your experiments.

Make sure that the test you intend to conduct fits your statement of purpose. Some students fail because of poorly-designed experiments and because of a mismatch between their tests and their original purpose.

Don't ignore data because it does not support your hypothesis. This can be especially tempting when you are in the latter stages of your work.

Don't ignore unsuccessful experiments. Analyse your findings, modify your hypothesis and write up everything you have done. You can still obtain good marks for experiments that yield unexpected results.

Do not be tempted to falsify tests and results because they are not producing the outcomes you expect. Tutors can spot when this has been done.

SUMMARY

This chapter has given advice and guidance on enhancing your mathematical and scientific skills. Many adults are worried about maths and science, but with a little practice and perseverance you will come to understand more about the subjects. By taking on board the tips offered in this chapter you will find that you are able to read and understand scientific material more effectively, understand and use graphs, charts and tables, cope with problem sheets and conduct experiments. However, if you are worried about your basic maths ability, you should seek help from the Study Support Unit (see Chapter 18) or contact the Basic Skills Agency for more information about courses in your area (see address at end of this book).

The next chapter provides advice and guidance for getting the most out of lectures and seminars.

(7)

Getting the Most out of Lectures and Seminars

On many courses you will be required to attend both lectures and seminars. Some courses that are run specifically for adults, however, will consist of much smaller groups and all classes will be taught following the 'seminar-style' format. This involves small groups of students and tutors getting together to discuss topics on the course. This chapter gives advice on getting the most out of seminars and from the more formal lectures experienced on most undergraduate courses.

PREPARING FOR LECTURES AND SEMINARS

It is important to prepare for lectures and seminars – it will help you to focus your mind and prepare yourself to receive information. Through careful preparation you can clear your mind and concentrate fully on the topic. You will also find that you are able to realise and build upon your existing knowledge of the subject. This will help you to retain the information more easily, especially when you begin to revise for examinations.

There are four main stages to the preparation process which should be carried out before your lecture or seminar:

1) Review your notes from previous lectures and/or seminars. Read through your notes and try to recall the main points.

2) Read more about the topic. This will help you to understand better the material covered and will help you to retain the information because it has more meaning.

3) Begin to form questions about the topic. Is there anything you don't understand? Is there anything that requires clarification? What do you want to know?

4) Predict what you think will be included in the lecture or seminar, based on your background reading and knowledge of the subject. What do you expect to be covered? What will be the main points?

Turn up early for your lecture or seminar so that you can choose a seat and location in which you are comfortable. This will help you to focus your mind on the topic.

IMPROVING LISTENING SKILLS

If you listen carefully you can learn more effectively and save yourself extra study time. Listening also enables you to find out what your tutor expects from you on the course. If you listen well you can pick up any clues that your tutor is offering about material to be included in assignments and examinations.

To improve your ability to listen well you need to do your preparation before the lecture and/or seminar. Through careful preparation the material will become more familiar and meaningful and listening will become easier. How often do you find yourself 'switching off' when listening to something that is complex and meaningless? If you have thought about what is to be included in the lecture, you will find it easier to concentrate.

Once in the lecture or seminar, the following points should help your listening to become more effective:

◆ Listen for the main points. Most good tutors will introduce their lecture with these main points and then summarise them in their conclusion.

◆ Listen willingly. Enjoy the lecture, note all the interesting points that are being made and try not to become distracted.

◆ Listen for clues about material to include in examinations and assignments. This will make your listening more active – you have a purpose for listening carefully and picking up on salient points. These clues may be given through what the tutor says and how they say it – their intonations, repetition, facial and hand gestures and volume and pitch of voice.

◆ When there is a pause in the main lecture, summarise what you have taken in so far.

◆ Try to hear what is being *said*, not what you want (or expect) to hear.

More tips on improving your listening skills can be found in Chapter 8.

IMPROVING AND MAINTAINING CONCENTRAION

As we have seen above, active listening helps you to maintain concentration. However, there are other things that you can do to help improve and maintain your concentration during lectures and seminars:

◆ Try to maintain the right frame of mind for study. Leave family problems or concerns at home if at all possible.

◆ Be aware of when your mind wanders to something other than the lecture. Pull your mind back to the subject.

◆ Don't just listen to what is being said, but try to understand it – form your own opinions or develop questions to aid your understanding. This will lead to deeper concentration.

◆ Avoid distractions – try to sit in a place that has the least distractions. In a lecture theatre this tends to be towards the front, in the middle.

◆ It is much harder to concentrate when you feel tired or under the weather. Try to remain fit and healthy and make sure that you get plenty of sleep.

TAKING NOTES EFFECTIVELY

It is impossible to remember everything that is said in a lecture or seminar, so you need to take notes to aid your memory. However, notes are effective only if you can understand them at a later date. To make sure that this is the case you need to think about your preparation, how you take notes, how you intend to organise your notes and your revision methods.

Preparation

Find out which style of notebook you prefer. Some students prefer the small shorthand notebook style, whereas others prefer A4 notebooks. Try out different types of pen or pencil – which type helps you to write quickly and comfortably?

Try to develop a shorthand style that you will remember – you might find it useful to produce a 'shorthand glossary' before you attend lectures. With practice you will find that this shorthand style becomes second nature. Don't change your shorthand style mid-way through the semester, however, as this will be confusing.

Prepare for the lecture. If you are aware of the topic and have read about the issues, you will find it easier to take notes.

Note-taking

During the lecture don't try to write down everything you hear. Instead, listen for the main points and make sure that these are included in your notes. Most people have to stop listening to write, so be selective about when you decide to write so that you don't miss any salient points.

Leave wide margins on either side of your notes. You can add extra information if the tutor returns to a previous point. You can also add extra information in the margins when you review your notes after the lecture. Use question marks to query any information of which you are unsure and to which you may need to return at a later date.

Visual aids are used to emphasise a point. Analyse carefully what you are being shown and take relevant notes, leaving gaps between them that you can fill in later. If you are listening actively you will find that questions are forming in your mind. You can jot these down and ask the tutor at the end of the lecture or search for the information yourself.

In maths and science subjects you might need to write down everything the lecturer writes on the board verbatim, as every symbol means something specific. Use diagrams to aid your understanding.

Be open-minded about any points on which you disagree – jot down a few notes to which you can return later, but do not become too distracted by your disagreement.

Organisation

Keep your notes well organised. When you attend a lecture or seminar write the subject, date and topic to be discussed at the top of the page and make sure that you begin each lecture with a new page.

After a lecture you may find that some notes need to be reorganised or rewritten if they are muddled. Summarise the main points of the lecture and include these with your lecture notes. File your notes and summaries with topics that cover the same or related areas. Have one file for each subject.

Revision

After each lecture or seminar it is important to review and organise your notes as this helps you to retain information. Also, if your notes are carefully organised you will find it easier to obtain material for assignments and to revise for examinations. It is best to do this as soon as possible after the lecture – the information will be fresh in your mind and you will be able to add additional information to your notes.

Once your lecture or seminar has finished, ask yourself the following questions:

1) What were the main points and/or argument?
2) What have I learned so far?
3) How does this relate to other lectures?
4) How does this relate to information I already know?
5) Are there any points about which I am unclear? If so, what am I going to do to clarify the point?

A useful tip is to talk to other students about the lecture. Go over the main points together and discuss any issues about which you are unsure. Or you could try to summarise the information as if you were going to explain the content of the lecture to someone who did not attend. Use the information you have learned – repeat it to others if possible and think about what you have learned when covering related subjects. All these things will help you to retain the information.

As you read through your notes, highlight any important information within the text. This will make it easier to skim-read at a later date. You may find it useful to repeat any important facts and figures in a summary at the end of your notes.

ASKING QUESTIONS

As you listen to your tutor, questions will begin to form in your mind. Write down these questions as you take notes so that you can remember them at a later date. Most tutors will let you know at the beginning of the course their stance on questions. Some tutors do not like to be interrupted during a lecture and ask that you reserve questions for the end of the session. Others are happy to take questions throughout the lecture, especially if they are from students who are listening actively.

In seminars you will be encouraged to ask questions. Don't be afraid to do so, however 'silly' you feel the questions might be – most tutors will be relieved that a student has asked anything at all. The aim of most seminars is to generate a free-flowing discussion in which all students can express their opinions and address any issues of which they are unsure.

SUMMARY

This chapter has given advice on getting the most out of lectures and seminars. Preparation is of particular importance – if you prepare thoroughly you are able to focus your mind and become more open to receiving information. Through developing your listening skills and freeing your mind from distraction, you will find that you are able to take in, and retain, information more effectively. Good note-taking is an important skill to develop – if your notes are comprehensive and well-organised it is much easier to find material for assignments and revise for exams.

To enhance your seminar skills further it is important to develop your group work skills. These are discussed in the following chapter.

8

Developing your Group Work Skills

On most courses you will be required to undertake some type of group work. This might be a group project for an assessed piece of work, or a group discussion on a particular topic.

Some people find group work a useful and enjoyable exercise, whereas other people find it a daunting and difficult task. This is because some people learn better in a group setting whereas others learn more effectively on their own (see Chapter 1), or it may be due to the make-up of the group and problems with disruptive group members.

By planning your group work and improving your personal team-work skills, you should find that working in a group can be a rewarding and valuable experience. This chapter provides advice and guidance on developing these skills.

IMPROVING YOUR COMMUNICATION SKILLS

Communication is the key to effective group work. It involves putting across your message effectively and listening to the opinions of other people.

Verbal Skills

Some people dread having to talk in front of other people. If this is the case with you, consult Chapter 14 where advice is given on conquering nerves when speaking in public.

When you are working in a group you need to be able to convey your thoughts and opinions effectively. You can do this by considering the following points:

◆ Explain your opinions clearly and concisely. Don't be afraid of pauses if they help you to structure your argument.

◆ Speak slowly – it's easier for you to follow your argument and easier for other people to listen.

◆ Don't take things personally when people don't agree with your opinions.

◆ Be patient – if someone doesn't seem to understand what you are saying, try explaining it in a slightly different way.

◆ Don't assume that you are right all of the time. Be open to other ideas and opinions. However, if you are certain of your views, don't be easily persuaded by alternative views, especially if they are expressed more forcefully than yours.

Listening Skills

How frustrated do you get when you know that someone is not listening to you, especially when you are saying something important or something that is close to your heart? But how do you know that they are not listening? What clues do they give to alert you to the fact that their mind is elsewhere or that they can't be bothered with your opinion?

Perhaps they don't make eye contact, or maybe they keep interrupting with their own thoughts and opinions. Do they try to guess what you are going to say, or walk away from you mid-sentence, leaving you annoyed and frustrated? If you think about the times you have felt that someone was not listening to you it will help you to improve your own listening skills.

In reality few of us listen well. Yet, good listening is an important skill to master and will help you with your studies, especially in your group work.

During your group work listening should be *active* rather than *passive*. You should be involved within the group – listening to other people, forming your own opinions and letting other people know what you think. You expect them to listen to you and you should listen to them. If the whole group is involved in active listening, the work of the group will run much more smoothly and be free from individual annoyance or frustration.

To help you to improve your active listening skills, consider the following points:

◆ Always make eye contact with the speaker – this shows that you are interested in what they are saying.

◆ Try not to be distracted when someone is speaking –

don't fiddle with a pen, look at what is happening outside the window or respond to others who are not speaking.

♦ When someone is speaking, take note of the *words* they are using and the *ideas* they are expressing. Start to distinguish between opinions, prejudice and fact.

♦ Make sure you let someone finish speaking – don't jump to conclusions about what they are going to say.

♦ Although it is acceptable to interrupt occasionally with a relevant question or opinion, don't do it too often or in a confrontational way – this will cause ill-feeling and may lead to other members of the group becoming defensive.

♦ If you agree with what someone has said, express your support and opinion. We all like to receive encouragement from others, especially if we are nervous or slightly unsure of what we are saying.

♦ If you are unsure of what someone is saying, ask questions. Try to ask *open* questions which start with words such as 'what', 'why', 'where' and 'how' as people cannot answer these with a simple yes or no and will have to elaborate on what they are saying.

Remember that other members of the group might be unconfident or nervous about speaking in a group setting. Give them a chance to speak and make sure that you, and other members of the group, listen to what they have to say.

In group work active listening has to be an activity undertaken by all members of the group for the group to work well. It may be useful to point this out at the beginning of the group – perhaps this could be included in a code of conduct (see below).

PLANNING YOUR GROUP WORK

When members of your group first meet you need to ask some initial questions:

◆ Do you need to appoint a chairperson? If so, how will this person be appointed?

◆ Do you need to keep a record of events, and if so, who will agree to do this?

◆ When, where and how regularly is your group going to meet?

◆ Is it possible and desirable to obtain contact details for each group member?

◆ Do you need somebody to keep track of time?

◆ How will you make sure that everybody in the group is able to make a contribution and that their opinions are not ridiculed or undervalued?

◆ Do people in your group have different strengths and weaknesses? How will you determine this and will it have an influence on the allocation of work?

◆ What work do you have to complete?

◆ How will your conclusions be presented and by whom?

As you probably have very little idea of how people will interact in your group, you can solve a lot of future problems by setting a few ground rules at the outset. When you first get together, work with your group to develop a 'code of conduct'. Make sure that every group member is happy with the code and agrees to abide by its rules. This could cover the following:

◆ The importance of actively listening to each other.

◆ Respecting individual values and opinions.

◆ Discouraging the use of offensive or upsetting language or opinions.

◆ The allocation of work and the commitment expected from each group member.

◆ What the group will do if someone doesn't turn up for meetings or doesn't complete their allocation of work.

◆ How you will resolve conflict if it arises.

◆ Issues of confidentiality – what should be kept inside the group?

The 'code of conduct' can be written on a flip chart or reproduced in a handout for each group member. If anyone strays from the rules, a gentle reminder from several group members may be enough to sort out the problem.

Some groups find it useful to produce a list of 'aims and objectives' or 'goals'. What do you want to get out of the group? What do you hope to achieve? How are you going to work together to achieve this outcome? Again, if a group member is not pulling their weight, a gentle reminder of the aims and objectives should help.

PRODUCING GROUP ASSIGNMENTS

If you have to produce a piece of assessed work make sure that everyone is clear about the deadline. Divide the work amongst group members – make sure everyone knows what they have to do and when it has to be completed. It might be useful to consider the strengths and weaknesses of each member – some will be good at research, others good at writing reports. Tasks can be allocated accordingly which will help motivation levels and improve the success of the group. Arrange regular meetings to keep track of what everyone is doing. In this way, if a group member is not doing their work, the problems can be detected early.

COPING WITH DIFFICULT GROUP MEMBERS

Every person in your group is different. They all have different personalities, different learning styles and different reasons for coming on the course. Despite this, everyone in your group is on your course and therefore has a common bond – most group members are interested in the subject and most will want to do well. However, there may be exceptions to this rule, and if you find that you are unlucky enough to have an unmotivated, disruptive member of your group, it can create trouble for the rest of you. The following points may help you to resolve problems in your group:

◆ Refer back to the 'code of conduct' and ask that everyone adheres to its rules.

◆ Talk the situation over as soon as it occurs. Don't let problems escalate.

◆ It is perfectly acceptable to *agree* to *disagree*. If someone is adamant about an issue and the work of the group is not moving forward, it might be better to leave the issue and move on to something else.

◆ If the group member is very disruptive and you can't solve the problems in your group, seek advice from your tutor. You can do this without mentioning names, although your tutor will probably know who you are talking about.

Although many groups work successfully and are not disrupted, some students do find themselves in an awkward position when undertaking group work. The following tips are from students who found themselves in such a predicament.

Student Tips – Disruptive Members

We had one person in the group who was a right pain. I don't know why he was on the course. He just wasn't interested in anything we were doing. He would not come to our meetings. He wouldn't do the work. In the end I decided to go to the tutor. I felt like I was squealing, but we were being marked on our work and it wasn't fair on the rest of us. The tutor told me that he had allocated this person to our group precisely for these reasons – he thought we might be able to pull him into shape. He said the student had problems and it would be good if we could try to help him a bit more. I went back to the group and told them. Two of us arranged a meeting and had a really long chat with him. It turned out he was nervous and shy – the way he acted was a complete front. We agreed to help him by never putting him on the spot, letting him choose what he wanted to do and asking him to arrange the meetings when it was best for him. You wouldn't believe how he changed. In the end he was one of the hardest-working people in the group. It's shown me not to jump to conclusions. **(Jeanne, 49)**

There was this one bloke who wouldn't listen to anyone else. He had his own political agenda and that is what he stuck to. He wasn't open to any other ideas or opinions. He was really disruptive – he would roll a cigarette in the meetings, even though he wasn't allowed to smoke. He would argue with everyone in a very confrontational way. We had to go to our tutor because we just couldn't get on with our work. She had a chat with him and he decided to leave the course – apparently it wasn't what he'd expected anyway. **(Peter, 41)**

There were two people in the group who weren't doing the work. As a group we decided to confront them. We were careful not to annoy them – we just tried to appeal to their better nature. It worked out for us and the group ran smoothly after that. I think I really improved my diplomacy skills as a result of being in that group. **(Nick, 27)**

ENHANCING YOUR GROUP EXPERIENCE

Group work can be a valuable and rewarding experience. To make sure that you get the most out of your group work, consider the following points:

◆ Develop a positive attitude towards group work.

◆ Be prepared to contribute and give your best.

◆ Get rid of prior expectations about group members.

◆ Don't get involved in gossip, take sides or be tempted to join factions.

◆ Recognise that everybody has different knowledge, skills and experiences. Don't be judgemental about these abilities.

◆ Keep an open mind – turn negative experiences into positive – what have you learned and how has it helped you to grow as a student?

◆ Recognise the valuable team-work skills and experience you have developed – communication skills, listening skills, negotiation, co-operation, delegation, conflict resolution, etc.

SUMMARY

This chapter has provided advice on how to develop your group work skills. Some adults work well in groups, others do not – it is all part of your particular learning style. Nevertheless, if you find that you do not work well in groups, there are several things that you can do to improve your experience. This includes improving your communication skills, planning your group work carefully and understanding how to cope with difficult group members. By taking on board the advice offered in this chapter you might discover that group work can be a valuable and rewarding experience.

The next chapter offers advice on mastering open and distance learning techniques.

9

Mastering Open and Distance Learning Techniques

With the rapid growth in the development and use of information technology, open and distance learning (ODL) is becoming an increasingly popular method of study, especially for those adults who are unwilling or too busy to attend a college or university. ODL includes any learning provision in which a significant part of the learning is managed by the learner and ranges from online learning to traditional correspondence courses.

However, ODL is not an easy option – to complete the course successfully an extra set of skills is required. These include the ability to learn as an individual without face-to-face contact; the need to build and maintain motivation without the support of other students; the ability to meet deadlines without constant reminders from tutors. ODL students must learn how to use a variety of self-instructional media and print materials, and they need to be organised and self-disciplined. This chapter provides advice on how to become an effective open and distance learner.

UNDERSTANDING AND USING INFORMATION TECHNOLOGY

To succeed on your ODL course you need to understand the technology you will be required to use. This may include television, videos, computers, CD-ROM, modems and the internet, e-mail, video-conferencing, electronic discussion forums and fax machines. Before you begin the course you will need to consider the following points:

◆ What equipment will you need to use? Will you have to purchase any new equipment? Can you afford to do so? Will you be able to set up the equipment yourself, and if not, who will do it for you and how much will it cost?

◆ What skills do you already possess? How do these match the course requirements? Are there any specific pieces of equipment with which you are unfamiliar? How do you intend to rectify this gap in your knowledge?

◆ Do you know anyone who can help install the equipment and train you in its use?

◆ Do you need to set any ground rules for other members of your family using the equipment? How will you ensure that videos will not be taped over or floppy disks wiped clean?

◆ What will you do if your equipment breaks down?

Chapter 10 provides advice on making the most of information technology. If you are new to computers it might be useful to enrol on a computing course before you begin your ODL course. This will help you to concentrate on your

studies rather than waste time trying to sort out technological problems. Some ODL centres will provide their
own IT induction courses which will prepare you for further
study.

When you work on your own you can spend hours trying to
solve a technological problem, when all you need is to be
told how to do it by someone who knows. You might not be
able to do this on ODL courses, so try to become familiar
with the technology before you begin your studies. The
following tips should help you to use information technology
more effectively:

◆ Consult the course literature and/or website as they
  should provide detailed guidelines about using the equipment required for the course. Some will run IT modules
  or induction courses.

◆ Check whether the college provides free technical
  referral and assistance.

◆ Make friends with somebody experienced in IT.

◆ Develop an online study group. You can use this group to
  gain support with your studies, but also to seek advice on
  technological problems.

◆ Practice using the equipment when you have plenty of
  time and are not constrained by deadlines.

◆ Remember the *help* button on your computer.

◆ The internet is a great source of information and advice
  for technological problems.

◆ Don't be embarrassed to ask your children for help – most will be proud to be of assistance.

◆ Keep all manuals carefully filed for easy reference.

◆ Remember to use any free IT support services that were offered when you purchased your equipment.

LEARNING AS AN INDIVIDUAL

Although tutorial support is available when required, most of the work you do as a distance learner will be carried out on your own, in your own time. This means that you have to be disciplined if you are to complete your studies successfully. In addition to working well independently, you will need to have the confidence to tackle complex concepts, ideas and arguments with little tutor input. Also, you will need to be able to understand, and follow, written instructions.

Some ODL courses will provide a timetable by which the various tasks should be completed. If a timetable is provided in this way, make sure that you adhere to it and complete all the tasks on time. If a timetable is not provided, you will need to produce your own. On a wall calendar note in red any important deadline and examination dates – if you are setting your own dates, make sure that you do not put yourself under any unnecessary pressure (see Chapter 3).

Once you have a visual representation of all the important dates and deadlines, you need to think about how much work you have to do to meet these deadlines. At the start of your course you may not know this because you don't yet know how easily or how quickly you can complete each module. For the first couple of weeks take note of how long tasks take. This will give you an idea of how much work you will need to complete each week to meet your deadlines. You can then produce a weekly timetable of tasks (see Chapter 2). Complete tasks early – don't leave things until the last minute as most tasks are much harder when you are working under pressure.

Many ODL courses provide self-assessment tests after each topic or class. Make sure that you complete these tests – they will act as a guide to how well you have understood the information. Don't be tempted to miss out the tests because you feel you do not have the time. If you find a test very hard, try it several times so that you understand what you are learning.

REMAINING MOTIVATED

Chapter 2 provides advice on building and improving motivation. For distance learning this is especially important. If you are to complete your course you have to keep your motivation levels high. In addition to the advice provided in Chapter 2, there are extra things that you can do to improve your levels of motivation:

◆ Choose a course and learning package in which you have a high level of interest.

◆ Poorly designed course materials can influence your levels of motivation. Check these before you start the course to make sure that they are well-designed and well-presented. Poor use of colour can be a de-motivator. However, if used properly colour can be a powerful tool to convey information – colour should be consistent, simple and clear. There should be plenty of 'white space' in the materials and they should look well-structured and uncluttered, with plenty of headings and sub-headings.

◆ Think about why you have chosen to study your course by distance learning. What are the main advantages? Pin this list in a prominent place and refer to it if you ever find yourself becoming frustrated with the method and technique of distance learning.

◆ Motivation levels can be influenced by problems of access to information and support. This includes access to libraries, student advisers, financial aid and technical support. Most ODL centres know that if they are to retain students they need to provide high levels of support. However, the onus is on you, as the student, to access this support. Make sure that you read the course literature carefully to find out what is available, and if in doubt, ask. Your tutor will be able to provide advice and guidance on what is available.

◆ Feelings of isolation influence motivation levels. Make sure that you participate in the course as much as possible – contact your tutor on a regular basis and contact other students whenever possible.

◆ Lack of feedback can influence motivation levels – if you feel you are receiving inadequate feedback, speak to your tutor.

◆ Low self-confidence can be a de-motivator. If you find yourself questioning your own ability to succeed, speak to your tutor.

OBTAINING BOOKS AND JOURNALS

Many ODL students study at a considerable distance from their college. If this is the case, you need to think about how you are going to access all the books and journals required to complete your work.

Many ODL centres have developed a postal loan service. Through this service books and photocopies of journals can be requested via the online catalogue and posted to your nominated address. Loan periods are often extended to include the time taken to post materials. However, many libraries will charge for this service and you will have to pay for return postage. If you use this service it is recommended that you use recorded delivery or obtain a certificate of posting when returning materials to guard against lost items.

The UK Libraries Plus scheme enables part-time, distance learning, full time postgraduate and placement students to borrow from the libraries of other higher education institutions. You can register to use up to three member institutions and can apply for borrower rights and reference access. For more information, including a list of members libraries and registration details see www.uklibrariesplus.ac.uk. To use host libraries you will need to present your identity card and the UK Libraries Plus registration form or membership card.

At the present time you will not have computer access at member libraries. However, a pilot scheme has been launched to test the possibility of opening up access to computers for distance learners. The project is called UK

Computing Plus and further details about this pilot study can also be obtained from the UK Libraries Plus website.

TIPS FOR SUCCEEDING AT DISTANCE LEARNING

Tutors and students on a variety of ODL courses were asked what they considered to be the most important pieces of advice to give students who wanted to succeed on their course. The tutor tips are as follows:

1) Make sure that you understand how the course is designed. Many courses offer a quiz or a questionnaire that you can complete before you enrol. This will enable you to find out whether the course meets your needs and is suited to your individual learning style.

2) Make sure that you have the minimum technical requirements for the course. Some ODL centres will provide you with a list of IT skills needed, or will ask you to complete a self-evaluation questionnaire prior to enrolment. If you don't have the right skills, enrol on a course to acquire them before you start your ODL course. As a tutor it can be quite frustrating to receive a barrage of questions about technology, rather than questions about the course content.

3) Read the course material and syllabus carefully so that you know exactly what the course is about and what is required.

4) Generate a strategy for successfully completing the course and stick to it. Set yourself targets to include the amount of time taken to complete a task, the quantity of work to be done in a week, progress through modules and progress through assignments.

5) If you are unsure about how to write an assignment, ask your tutor to supply you with a copy of a good assignment. Most tutors have plenty to choose from.

6) If you are struggling with something, move onto something new. Make a note of your problems and speak to your tutor or other students. Don't stop working just because one topic is holding you up.

7) You will receive a lot of course material. Don't try learning it all – some topics will need you only to understand the issues. Try to distinguish between what has to be *learned* and what should be *understood*.

8) Make contributions and share your ideas with tutors and other students.

9) Check your e-mail and post regularly and don't get behind with your work.

10) Apply what you have learned. Even better, try to practice what you have learned – you will find it easier to retain the information.

11) Organise your time effectively – many ODL courses provide advice and guidance on time management (see Chapter 3).

12) Find a suitable place to study.

13) Go over a piece of work until you thoroughly understand it.

14) Speak to your tutor if you have any problems. Tutors are there to help and will do everything they can to get you through your course.

The box below lists the student tips on succeeding at distance learning.

Succeeding at Distance Learning – Student Tips

Form an online study group with other students. I found it invaluable to discuss things I was struggling with, especially assignment topics that were hard to understand. It also stops you feeling so isolated. **(Alison, 39)**

If you have bought your textbooks mark them with pencil as you read. Highlight important areas that you can return to, or put question marks by things you don't understand. This makes it easier to review the books for exams and assignments. I also heard somewhere that it helps you to learn if you add personal notes to course materials. **(Robert, 28)**

If you are really not in the mood to work, don't force yourself. It can make it really hard going and you might start to dislike your subject. Wait until you are in the mood and you will find that your work flows much easier and you enjoy what you are doing. **(Rosemary, 32)**

I decorated the spare room in a calming lilac colour. Then I bought a new desk, chair and filing cabinet. I filed all my work somewhere where it could be found easily and I forbade anyone else to enter the room. It was my sanctuary. I knew when I was in that room I would be able to concentrate and not be disturbed. It was calming and I found I was much more productive. **(Jennifer, 53)**

I found it really useful to work quickly through areas I found easy or familiar. Then I would have much more time available to spend on those areas that I found hard or confusing. **(Nigel 27)**

Don't work when you are tired or constantly being distracted. It is really hard to do and you don't retain the information. Wait until you're wide awake and there are no distractions – you can do twice as much, twice as quickly. **(Angie, 37)**

UTILISING TUTOR FEEDBACK

To be a successful ODL student you need to use tutor feedback effectively. On many courses you will not meet your tutor face-to-face, but instead will receive written feedback, either through the post or via e-mail. When you receive this type of written feedback you cannot tell in what context it has been written – whether the tutor was happy or annoyed, pleased or dismayed with your work. It is easy to take comments out of context and read much more into them than was ever intended by the tutor. This is especially true with tutors who have a brief, 'straight-to-the point' style.

When you receive feedback try to keep your emotions away from what you are reading. Take the comments for what they are – constructive advice about what you have done well, what has not been done so well and what can be improved upon. Try not to take any criticism personally, but instead relate it to your work and future assignments.

Sometimes, however, you may find that you are unsure about what is being said. If this is the case, contact your tutor and ask for clarification. Think about how you word your correspondence and try not to be confrontational or accusing – remember that your tutor will not know how you were feeling when you communicated. Remember also that it is useful for tutors to receive feedback on the usefulness and clarity of their feedback! More advice on dealing with tutor feedback is offered in Chapter 17.

SUMMARY

This chapter has offered advice on mastering open and distance learning techniques. ODL is becoming an increasingly popular method of study, especially for adults who are unable to attend classes at a college or university. Although ODL can be much more flexible than other modes of study, students can encounter extra problems and pressures. This may include problems with equipment, learning as an individual, feelings of isolation, lack of motivation, problems with obtaining materials and dealing with tutor feedback. This chapter has offered guidance for overcoming these difficulties.

The following chapter will go on to consider information and communication technology. The advice offered in the next chapter will be of benefit to all distance learners.

Making the Most of Information and Communication Technology

As a student you should try to use computers as much as possible. They will make it easier for you to write and complete your assignments; they enable you to carry out in-depth research without leaving your seat; they can perform complex data analysis; they can help you to draw professional-looking graphs and charts.

If you are a beginner try not to be afraid of computers. The technology may seem advanced – you may think it is too complex and beyond your comprehension. But computers are like any new technology – a little practice, patience and perseverance and you will wonder how you ever lived without them.

This chapter provides advice and guidance on making the most of information and communication technology. Please note that, as the majority of students use Microsoft products, the advice provided in this chapter is related to these products. If your college or university uses other products, seek advice from your Computer Services help desk.

GETTING STARTED

If you have never used a computer before, visit the Computer Services department at your college or university. Most of these departments will provide information packs for people who are new to computers, or unconfident about their use. Find out whether the department runs training courses for beginners and enrol on a course. You will find it useful to meet with other students who are in your position, and it is reassuring to know that you are not alone. The tutors will help you to get started and enable you to practice on a computer with all the help and support you need.

If your college does not provide this facility ask a friend, another student or even your children to help you get started. Once you have been shown the basics you will find that practice and experimentation is the best way to learn, and you might be surprised at how quickly you pick up the information.

WRITING ON A COMPUTER

In most colleges and universities students are expected to word process their assignments, projects and dissertations. If you are new to computers you may find it hard to believe that writing on a computer can be more effective and much easier than writing long-hand. This is for the following reasons:

◆ You can lay out your work in a professional manner (although content and structure is important, a professionally-laid out piece of work will attract more marks).

◆ Your tutor will be able to read your work easily and not struggle with your handwriting.

◆ There are many features available to personalise your work, e.g. different typefaces and sizes, borders and shading, indentation, different types of headings, sub-headings and footers, different margins and so on.

◆ A good word processing package will help you with your grammar and your spelling, although you must never rely completely on this facility.

◆ You can *cut* and *paste* which means that you can change the order of your paragraphs, sentences or words at the touch of a button.

◆ You can add graphs, charts and tables to your work.

◆ If you learn to type you can produce your assignments more quickly.

PRODUCING A DOCUMENT

Students produce their work in different ways. Someone who is unfamiliar with computers may decide to write their work in long-hand first and then type-up the finished version using the computer. This is a method which may suit someone who has not used computers before, but it can be a time-consuming and lengthy process. Most students find that they are much better composing their assignments on the computer.

There are two main ways that students do this:

◆ All the ideas are typed in as quickly as possible. A large amount of editing, layout, style and presentation is needed at the end, using cut and paste and text-changing functions.

◆ Careful and lengthy preparation at the beginning means that the text is carefully entered in a logical, systematic way, with layout, style and presentation carried out simultaneously. Only a small amount of editing is needed at the end.

The method you choose will depend upon your learning style, or you may find that you alternate between the two depending upon the subject of the assignment and as you become more familiar with the computer.

Some students who have real trouble typing may prefer to use voice dictation software. This can be particularly useful for students with dyslexia. If you think that this might help you, speak to staff at your Computer Services Helpdesk who will be able to offer advice.

Below are some tips to help you when producing documents on a computer.

Writing a Document – Tips

1) When you read documents written by other people, take note of their layout and design. What do you like? What doesn't look good? Remember these features when you come to write your own documents.

2) Be consistent in your page design – keep the same-sized margins, headers and footers throughout your document.

3) Don't use too many fonts or typefaces. The two most popular are Times New Roman and Arial.

4) The most common font size is 12 point.

5) Don't make your lines of text too long – graphic designers recommend a line of text between 8 and 20 words wide.

6) Don't use the *underline* facility too often as it can chop off the tails of letters and look cluttered. Try using *bold* or *italic* instead.

7) Use an indent or a blank line between paragraphs, but don't use both. Either will do, but make sure that you are consistent throughout your document.

8) Use visual aids in your document if they help to express your ideas or if they would have more impact than words. But don't use visual aids for the sake of it and don't waste too much time producing a perfect chart or graph when it is not completely relevant.

PRINTING YOUR WORK

Once you have completed a draft of your work, use the *print preview* button to check that you are happy with the layout of the document. This can be found near the *print* command on the *file* menu.

Once you are happy with your layout, you should always print a draft copy of your work before you print a final copy. This is for the following reasons:

◆ It is often easier to spot spelling, typing and grammatical mistakes when you have a hard copy of the document. You may find it easier to proofread a hard copy of your work.

◆ Certain aspects of your layout and page design may not print properly. Some printers may change the position of the text and some fonts may not be available on the printer you use. You will need to check that your document prints in the manner you intend.

◆ Most colleges and universities will allow you to print draft copies of your work free of charge. If you spot something you wish to change you will not have wasted any money.

When you are happy with your work and feel there is nothing left to alter, print your final copy on a good quality printer.

FILE MANAGEMENT

When you have written a document on the computer you need to save your work so that you can retrieve the document another time. You will notice an icon at the top of your screen that looks like a floppy disk (hold your curser over each icon if you are not sure which to choose). Using the left button on your mouse, click once on this icon – you will be asked where you want to save your document. You will need to think of an appropriate name for your document. When you are organising your documents on the computer, keep it simple. That way you will be able to locate your work more easily.

When you save a document that you have written it is called a *file*. Each assignment will be saved as a file and will need a *file name*. Gradually, as you complete more work, you will create more and more files. Rather than have a long list of files it is easier to organise your files into specific groups. These are called *folders* and you will need to name each folder.

The way that you organise your documents is an individual process and with practice you will find a method that best suits you. However, from research with new students, the following method was found to be the most popular and effective.

◆ **Step 1** – Use *Windows Explorer* to organise your files and folders. To access this software click on Start → Programs → Accessories → Windows Explorer.

◆ **Step 2** – Create a folder for each of the subjects or modules on your course. To do this, when you are in Windows Explorer click on File → New → Folder.

◆ **Step 3** – Name each of the folders. Keep it simple. Many students use the name of the course such as 'Geography', 'Sociology' and so on.

◆ **Step 4** – Once you have written an assignment you need to save it to the right location. Click on the floppy disk icon on your menu bar. The first time you do this a box will pop-up on your screen. Choose the appropriate folder in the box at the top where it says *save in*. For example, if the assignment is the first piece of work for Geography, it would be saved in the Geography folder.

◆ **Step 5** – Give the file an appropriate name, such as 'assignment1.doc' (depending on what software you are using you may need to put '.doc' after your file name). Enter this name in the box at the bottom of the screen where you are asked for *file name*. Then click on *save*.

◆ **Step 6** – Once you have saved your work in this way, remember to regularly click on the save button as you add more text. Your work will be saved in the right location without you having to repeat the above process.

BACKING UP FILES

'Backing up' your work means that you make copies of what you have done so that, should anything happen to your computer, you will not lose all of your valuable work. Backing up your work is an important habit that you should develop as soon as you start using a computer. Consider the following examples:

Jean (27)

I was just finishing my first assignment. It had caused me no end of trouble, mainly because I was unsure of how to structure it and didn't quite know what should go into it, but also because I was unfamiliar with the computer. Then we had a power cut. I had been struggling on the assignment for four days and suddenly all my work was lost. I couldn't believe it. I just burst into tears.

Robbie (24)

My computer decided to give up the ghost one day. I had three different pieces of work on the computer and I couldn't get at anything. I lost all of them and there was nothing I could do. One of my mates had been telling me to back up everything I did but I just hadn't listened to him. As you can imagine, I've learnt from my mistakes – I will never do that again.

These examples show how important it is to back up any work that you do on the computer. If you have a copy of your work stored at a different location, you will always have a copy should anything happen to the original copy.

When you are composing on screen save your work every five or ten minutes. That way you will not lose much information if you experience a power cut or other problems with your computer. At the end of the day, back up all the work you have done that day onto floppy disk, CD or the university network. It is better not to rely solely on floppy disks because they can be unreliable.

Start as you mean to go on – if saving and backing up your work becomes habit, you will never forget.

USING THE INTERNET

The internet is a vast array of information from all around the world on almost every subject imaginable. You can find information on virtually any topic without getting up from your seat. Anyone can post information on the internet about any subject that interests them. Some of the information will be useful, some will be misleading and some will be offensive. To take full advantage of the information on offer, you need to know how to surf the net efficiently and how to critique the information that you have found (see Chapter 12).

The Internet at College

All students can access the internet at their college or university, free of charge. However, some learning providers may limit the amount of time that you can spend on the internet and others will limit the amount of space you are given to store the information you have downloaded. All learning providers will have strict rules about obscene material, software theft and breach of copyright or plagiarism.

When you first start your course, visit the Computer Services department or their website and pick up a list of the rules and regulations for using the internet. Most Computer

Services will provide you with information about how to use the internet.

The Intranet at College

Many colleges and universities have an 'intranet' – an internal computer network which contains information of use to students and staff at that institution. This may include course notes, student and staff notice boards, health and safety information, access to the library, examples of examination papers, local events and information for students with disabilities. Contact your Computer Services department for more information.

USING E-MAIL

If you are new to computers you should familiarise yourself with the *electronic mail* (e-mail) system as soon as possible, as increasingly tutors and students are using the system to exchange important information and messages. Tutors can send one message to all their students at the touch of a button, and they will expect all their students to read, respond or react to the message.

Before you can start to send and receive e-mail messages you will need your own e-mail address. When you enrol on your course contact staff at the Computer Services department who will issue you with an e-mail address for their system. You may also be given a login name and password – for identification and security purposes – which you need to remember in addition to your e-mail address.

Using the Internet and E-mail Effectively – Student Tips

Read the hints and tips offered by *Google* (www.google.co.uk). They really help you to search for information more effectively. **(Jeanette, 45)**

Remember to note the web page and date you found the information if you're going to use it in your work. You will need it for your bibliography and it's really hard and a waste of time to try and retrace your steps on the net. **(Joe, 38)**

Don't get involved in sending chain e-mails. They are a complete waste of time and clog up your mail box. Tell your friends not to send them to you. **(Alison, 39)**

I find it useful to have two e-mail accounts – one that I keep solely for university messages and one for personal messages. **(Louise, 24)**

The best time to surf the net is in the morning when America has yet to go online. Your searches will be a lot quicker at this time. **(Penny, 28)**

Remember to add any interesting sites to your list of 'favourites'. You always think you will remember the page, but you never do. Also, remember the *history* button if you want to retrace your steps. **(Pete, 31)**

> Always write down websites as soon as you hear them and think they will be useful. Write it down carefully – there's nothing more frustrating than not finding a site because you have put one letter in the wrong place. **(Simon, 24)**
>
> Don't do anything you shouldn't be doing on the campus network – the computer technicians will find out about it. **(Colin, 29)**
>
> Don't give your e-mail address to any dodgy sites – you will receive loads of unwanted mail which will fill up your mail box and probably send you loads of viruses. **(Robbie, 24)**

AVOIDING VIRUSES

Computer viruses are malicious programmes developed by people who tend to have too much time on their hands. They are designed to annoy their recipients and cause all sorts of problems to our computers.

Viruses are spread from infected files loaded onto our computers. This is done usually in three ways:

◆ when we load files from infected floppy disks

◆ when we download files from the internet

◆ when we open an infected e-mail

If you undertake any of the above activities your computer is at risk from infection. To reduce this risk you should make sure that you purchase anti-virus software and you should update this software on a regular basis so that it can detect and clear the newest viruses. Some anti-virus software will automatically remind you to update. When obtaining software, take advantage of educational discounts and free software offered to students (see Chapter 18).

You should try to get into the habit of regularly scanning your computer for viruses. Some viruses can lie dormant for a long time – you might think that your computer is working normally, but the virus could be causing trouble behind the scenes. Any files that you load onto your computer, whether this is from a floppy disk, the internet or e-mail attachments, should be scanned for viruses.

If you find that you have got a virus, don't panic. Most will be detected and cleared by your anti-virus software, if it is regularly updated. If a virus is not cleared, you can find more information about it on the internet – some websites will enable you to download a programme that will clear your computer of the virus.

Make sure that you back up all your files at regular intervals. That way you will have copies of your work should you lose anything due to a virus.

SUMMARY

Some adult students are nervous about using information technology, especially if they have not used the equipment before. However, using computers can make your life as a student much easier and it is therefore important to come to terms with the equipment available. This chapter has provided advice on how to get started on computers, save, store and retrieve information, use the internet and e-mail, produce documents and avoid viruses.

More advice about searching for information on the internet is provided in Chapter 12. The next chapter will go on to provide advice and guidance for producing successful assignments.

Producing Successful Assignments

Producing your first assignment can be a daunting process, especially when you haven't had to produce this type of written work before. If you are nervous about writing your first assignment, have a chat with your personal tutor. They will be able to help you with any individual problems and offer advice about what should be included in the assignment. If they have time, they might be happy to look at a draft version before you hand in the final assignment for assessment.

Find out when deadlines for assignments are due and begin writing early – that way you will not put yourself under undue pressure trying to meet your deadlines. This chapter provides advice and guidance to help you to produce successful assignments.

STAGES OF THE WRITING PROCESS

If you are new to writing assignments you will find it useful to break down the procedure into a series of stages. That way the process is much less daunting and you can logically work through each stage until your assignment is complete.

As you become more familiar with writing assignments you may find that the order of the stages listed below changes slightly. You may also find that you are able to carry out some of the tasks simultaneously.

Before you start an assignment, find out from your tutor whether you are required to produce the work within a certain number of words or pages as this will help you to get an idea of how much material should be included.

Stage 1 – Choose a Topic
On some courses you will only be given one topic, in which case the choice is already made for you. If, however, you are presented with a list of topics, you must decide which you wish to discuss. When choosing a topic don't waste too much time making your decision. Look at each topic in turn and jot down a few points about each – this will give you an indication about your current knowledge, what your interests are and the topics that you know nothing about.

If this is your first assignment you might feel more comfortable choosing a topic about which you already have some knowledge – this will help your confidence. However, as you progress on your course, do not dismiss topics that you think you know nothing about. These can be interesting to research and will help to keep your motivation levels high.

Some students prefer to avoid general topics because it is harder to decide what material should be included. More specific topics help you to direct your reading and refine your argument. You will find that there is enough reading material available on what appear to be very specific topics.

Stage 2 – Understand what is being asked

Make sure that you understand what the question is asking. Read it several times so that you are clear. You might find it useful to discuss the question with other students to make sure that you have interpreted it correctly. If you are really unsure, try to arrange a meeting with your tutor to discuss the question in more depth.

Stage 3 – Identify key areas

Once you have chosen your topic, identify a number of key areas which will help to direct your background reading. These key areas may change as your reading progresses, but this initial list will help you to identify important texts.

Stage 4 – Begin your reading

In the early stages of your reading you may find it useful to identify a more general text that helps you to consider the overall question and topic. This will help you to start developing ideas for more specific reading.

Stage 5 – Take notes

As soon as you begin reading start taking notes. As you read, write down the main points and issues which relate to the question. Collect facts as well as opinions. Start organising your notes immediately – do not leave this until you have scribbled pages and pages of notes as they will be harder to organise. By organising your notes from the start you will be able to make sure that you only make notes relevant to the question. Remember to write down the bibliographical details of *every* book you read, and always note page numbers of relevant pieces or quotations that you might use in your assignment. Bibliographical details should include:

◆ Author's surname and initials;

◆ Date of publication;

◆ Title of the book;

◆ Publisher;

◆ Place of publication;

◆ Page numbers of specific information or quotations.

If you are reading a journal you will need to note the following:

◆ Author's surname and initials;

◆ Title of the article;

◆ Title of the journal;

◆ Volume and/or number of the journal;

◆ Page numbers of the article within the journal.

If you are obtaining information from a website you need to note the following:

◆ Author's surname and initials (if known);

◆ Date of publication or last revision;

◆ Title of document;

◆ Title of complete work (if relevant);

◆ URL/web address;

◆ Date of access.

You must remember to note all these details at the time of accessing the information – it can be very difficult and time-consuming to retrace your reading at a later date.

Stage 6 – Follow-up reading

By now you should be getting a feel for what is relevant reading matter. You can follow up your general reading with specialist reading such as journal articles or conference papers. Use the bibliographies of books that you have found useful to help steer you in a more specialised direction. When you write your assignment you should include information from a variety of sources – this will show that you have covered the topic well.

Stage 7 – Develop arguments

As you read you will find that you begin to form ideas about the topic. Write these down as soon as you think of them – you will find that some or all of these ideas can be used in your assignment. As you start to develop your own ideas you will find that arguments form in your mind. You will then be able to return to the reading to find evidence to support your arguments. Your arguments can serve three different purposes:

◆ They can defend a claim.

◆ They can answer a question or provide a solution to a problem.

◆ They can explore an idea or a claim without taking a stand.

The purpose of your argument will depend upon the nature of your assignment. In most cases you will be required to answer a question and back up your answer with evidence from relevant literature. Remember to note bibliographical details and page numbers of any evidence you intend to use. If you find that your argument is not developing easily you could try some exploratory writing, brainstorming the issues or more in-depth reading.

Stage 8 – Begin to develop your main argument

By now your main argument should be developing. Take a little time to work through this argument, finding evidence from your notes to support your ideas. You may decide that you have enough information available, or you may feel that you need to return to your reading for more evidence.

Stage 9 – Return to the question

Once you have developed your main argument, return to the question to check that you are sticking to the topic and have not got side-tracked with irrelevant information.

Stage 10 – Organise your notes and argument

Once you are happy that you are answering the question with your main argument, you can begin to organise your notes and argument into a coherent, logical structure. This will help you when you begin to write. Divide the work into manageable chunks and think about introductory sentences for each section. You could try brainstorming a few sentences and choosing the best.

Some people find it useful to transfer relevant arguments, facts and opinions onto cards and then order the cards into a logical structure. Other people find it useful to draw a diagram or a pictorial representation of how all the parts of their argument fit together.

Stage 11 – Write a draft introduction

Beginning to write can be daunting, but don't put it off. Just start writing – this is only a draft and you can alter it at a later stage. You will find that you feel better about your work when you have something, whatever standard, in writing. Your introduction should begin with a general statement – try brainstorming a few and choose the one you like best. The introduction should do the following:

◆ Identify the key points in relation to the topic.

◆ Provide a brief answer to the question, or a summary of your argument.

◆ Provide a plan on how the question will be answered.

Some people find it easier to write their introduction after they have written the main part of the assignment.

Stage 12 – Write a draft main section

This section should follow the points set out in the introduction. It should contain your argument backed up by evidence on each of the points you are discussing. Any evidence you use should be well-referenced. Don't use the words or arguments of others and try to pass these off as your own. This is plagiarism and your tutor will be able to spot this easily. Use transition sentences to move from one paragraph or one argument to the next. You can do this by repeating key words or ideas.

Stage 13 – Write a draft conclusion

This should sum up your argument and leave the reader in no doubt about the answer to the question. End your assignment with a general statement. Again, you can try brainstorming a few and then choosing the best.

Stage 14 – Produce the references and bibliography

The reference section includes all the literature to which you have referred in your assignment. Find out which referencing system your college or university uses. A popular method is the Harvard system which lists the authors' surnames alphabetically, followed by their initials, date of publication, title of book in italics, place of publication and publisher. If the reference is a journal article, the title of the article appears in inverted commas and the name of the journal appears in italics, followed by the volume number and pages of the article.

If you have read other publications but not actually referred to them when writing your assignment, you should include them as a bibliography at the end of your assignment. However, make sure that they are still relevant to your work – including books to make your bibliography look longer and more impressive is a tactic which won't impress tutors.

At this present time there are a variety of methods used for referencing information obtained from the internet. Ask your tutor which method is preferred at your college or university and remember to record all the information you require at the time that you access a particular website.

Stage 14 – Review the draft

Read through your draft assignment, picking up on any weak points in your argument and any problems that you may have with the structure. You may find that you have to return to your reading if you have missed out anything important. Some tutors, if they have time, will be happy to comment on a draft assignment and suggest alterations for your final version.

At this stage, check that all your references in the main text are correct. These should appear as the author's surname, the date of publication and page number in brackets positioned after the relevant quotation or piece of text, for example (Dawson, 2002: 44).

Stage 15 – Re-draft your assignment

Re-write your assignment, altering the structure and content if required and checking that all references are clear. Make sure that your assignment is within the required word or page limit.

Stage 16 – Edit and proofread

Once you are happy with your draft assignment in terms of content and structure you need to go through your work checking for grammatical errors and spelling mistakes. Don't rely on your computer to do this – you will find that certain mistakes aren't corrected.

Some students find it useful to leave their work for a couple of days, if they have time, and then proofread. This is because they can approach the work with a fresh mind and spot mistakes that they may have missed previously. Try to read each word individually – it will help you to spot mistakes. When you read quickly you assume that the words are right and you will find it more difficult to spot errors.

Reading your assignment out loud will help you to find out whether it flows well. This is because you are hearing the words as well as seeing them. Some students find it useful to work with a friend and proofread each other's assignment – it can be more difficult to detect mistakes in your own work than it is to detect mistakes in someone else's work.

DEVELOPING A CONCISE WRITING STYLE

On most courses you will be required to complete your assignments within a specified amount of words. Don't be tempted to produce more than the maximum amount of words in the hope that you will receive more marks because this will not be the case. Indeed, some tutors will penalise you heavily for exceeding the maximum word count.

To produce successful assignments you will need to cultivate a concise writing style that will enable you to pack as many ideas and arguments into your assignment as possible. The following tips will help you to do this:

◆ Keep the audience and purpose of your work in mind.

◆ Prioritise the main points that you wish to include. Go through your list making sure that all of these points are relevant before you begin to write. You will receive higher marks if you are able to show that you can discriminate between relevant and irrelevant information.

◆ Keep sentences short and make sure that your paragraphs are not too long.

◆ Only use quotations if they are relevant and help to explain a point that you are making. Do not include irrelevant material, however interesting it is to you. Stick to the question. When you read a draft version of your assignment, make sure that every part of your writing is relevant and cut it out if this is not the case.

◆ In some subjects, such as Mathematics and Science, don't use words when a table or diagram would better illustrate your ideas (see Chapter 6).

TIPS FOR IMPROVING MARKS

The following tips have been provided by tutors who regularly mark students' work:

◆ Make sure that your work is neatly presented and free from grammatical errors and spelling mistakes.

◆ Pay particular attention to the structure – your introduction should flow nicely into the main section and onto the conclusion.

◆ Make sure that you answer the question and keep your work free from irrelevant material.

◆ Back up all your arguments with *relevant* evidence.

◆ Do not use other peoples' words and arguments – it is so easy to spot when you do this.

◆ The secret to good writing is rewriting. Always produce a

draft, rewrite and then rewrite again. Even the best writers review their work.

◆ Writing is not a talent reserved for a select few – it is a skill that can be learned – ask your tutor, read books, learn the skill. Remember the saying 'practice makes perfect'!

◆ Keep ideas together that belong together. Don't change your ideas or arguments mid-paragraph.

◆ Avoid long, complex sentences and terminology that you don't understand. Tutors know when you are trying to impress but don't really know what you are talking about.

◆ Hand in your work on time. Don't come out with lame excuses about why your work is late – only in exceptional circumstances will you be given an extension. However, courses aimed specifically at adults might have more flexibility. Speak to your tutor if you find that you are having difficulty with deadlines.

Overcoming Writer's Block

Have a break and return to your work when you feel refreshed. Divide your work into short periods.

Put together your bibliography or references – you are still working but you won't be affected by writer's block.

Write part of your assignment as a diary entry or a letter to a friend. It may help the words to flow and you can then rewrite when you feel up to it.

Don't be afraid to write in the wrong order – if you are struggling move on to something else. This is no problem when you use the cut and paste facility on your computer.

Brainstorm each section of your assignment as a list and return to it when you feel comfortable writing.

Write a draft, however bad. You could even try to make it bad. It will amuse you and will help ideas to flow.

SUMMARY

Many adult students are concerned about producing assignments, especially if they have not undertaken this type of written work before. However, if you break the task down into a series of steps you will find that the process becomes a lot easier. This chapter has provided advice on how to do this. Some students will find that, as their course progresses, they are able to miss out some of these steps, or carry out other steps simultaneously.

Being able to conduct efficient and effective research is crucial to producing good assignments, projects and dissertations. The next chapter offers advice and guidance on carrying out both primary and secondary research.

$$\binom{12}{}$$

Mastering Research
Techniques

On most courses you will be required to undertake some type of research for your studies. This may be a small piece of research for a group project, or it may be a major piece of research for an undergraduate dissertation. Also, you will have to undertake research in the form of literature and information searches in your library and on the internet. This chapter offers advice and guidance on conducting effective research for your studies.

PRIMARY AND SECONDARY RESEARCH

As a student you may be required to undertake two types of research – *primary research* and *secondary research*. Primary research involves the study of a subject through firsthand observation and investigation, such as interviewing people or searching through statistical data. Secondary research involves the collection of information from studies that other researchers have made of a subject, such as research papers published in journals or on the internet. The different sources of primary and secondary research are listed below.

SOURCES OF BACKGROUND INFORMATION

PRIMARY
Relevant people
Researcher observation
Researcher experience
Historical records/texts
Company/organisation records
Personal documents (diaries, etc.)
Statistical data
Works of literature
Works of art
Film/video
Laboratory experiments

SECONDARY
Research books
Research reports
Journal articles
Articles reproduced online
Scientific debates
Critiques of literary works
Critiques of art
Analyses of historical events

As most students find that they have to undertake secondary research before they conduct primary research, this chapter will begin by discussing secondary research.

HOW TO CONDUCT SECONDARY RESEARCH

As you noticed in the previous chapter, when you are asked to complete an assignment you will need to begin by collecting information to help you to develop your arguments. This information is most commonly found in your college or university library, or on the internet.

Using the Library

The best way to become familiar with your library is to make sure that you go on the library tour arranged by your tutor at the beginning of your course. The librarians will show you the different sections of the library. This could include the reference section, short loan section, journals and periodicals, study areas, archives, newspapers and magazine section. You will also be shown how to use the library catalogue system. If you are unable to attend a tour, some tips for using your library catalogue appear in the box below.

Using Library Catalogues

Systems may differ slightly, but in general you should be able to do the following:

Log on to the system. You will need a library card number and password to do this. Some systems will enable you to set some personal parameters that will help you each time you search for information. This can include the amount of records you would like to have displayed after each search.

Perform a quick search. This will enable you to type your search terms and choose the field from a drop-down menu. You can search by keyword, title, author, subject, journal title and ISBN.

Perform a full search. This enables you to carry out a more specific search, combining a number of search terms. You can search the same terms as above, but combine them for more specific and accurate results.

Consult the display screen. Your search results will appear on screen and you can work through the list, checking or clicking on those that interest you. When you do this more details about the book will be displayed, including details about where the book can be found and whether it is out on loan. Some systems will enable you to store your search results for the duration of your session.

E-mail your results to yourself. If you wish to keep your results, some systems will enable you to send yourself an e-mail.

Review your search history. Some systems will enable you to do this when you next log on to the system. This is a useful facility if you want to retrace your search steps.

Put in a hold request. If you are interested in an item that is on loan, you can request a copy. If the book is popular you will be held in a queue which you will move up gradually. You can check your progress through the catalogue system. You can also request items from the library that are not on open access, such as those from basement stacks.

Renew your library books. Most libraries will enable you to renew your books through the catalogue system, usually up to four times if they have not been requested by other borrowers.

Log off the system. You need to remember to log off when you have finished, although most systems will log off automatically after a certain period of inactivity.

Your library may offer an *Interlending and Document Supply* service which means that you can access books, journals, maps and other documents from other university libraries if they are not available in your library. Most libraries will place a limit on the amount of requests you are allowed to make through this service. For more information about college and university libraries see Chapter 18.

Researching on the Internet

The information available on the internet is unstructured – there is no central index or contents page to help you to find what you are looking for. Instead there are four main ways to find information on the internet:

◆ Find out the web address and enter it in the 'address' box on your browser. If the web page is not found, check that you have typed the address correctly.

◆ Think of keywords and enter them in the 'search' box on your search engine. There are a variety of search engines available – you will soon find that you prefer some to others and that some are more efficient than others (see below).

◆ Follow the headings and links offered by your preferred search engine. Click on each heading to refine your search.

◆ Follow the links which take you to other sites that may be relevant to your original search.

Useful Search Engines

Google (http://www.google.co.uk)   Lycos (http://www.lycos.co.uk)

Yahoo! (http://www.yahoo.com)   Alta Vista (http://uk.altavista.com)

Excite (http://www.excite.co.uk)   Ask Jeeves (http://www.ask.co.uk)

InfoSeek Guide   Mirago
(http://infoseek.go.com)   (http://www.mirago.co.uk)

Think about your learning style (see Chapter 1) – this will help you to get the most out of the internet. Do you like to begin a project by brainstorming ideas and then searching out the literature that helps you to develop these ideas? If this is the case, use your brainstorm list to develop keywords that can be entered into the search bar. You will then be presented with a list of sites with information that may help you to develop your key ideas.

Or perhaps you prefer to go to the literature first and develop your ideas from what you read? If this is the case, try surfing the net by going to one site and following the links to another and then on to another. The information you come across may help you to develop and refine your ideas.

Whichever method you adopt, be disciplined – many student hours are wasted each day when people get side-tracked when surfing the net. Keep focused and stick to the task.

When you are surfing the net, there are some precautions you can take to check the reliability and quality of the information you have found:

◆ Try to use websites run by organisations that you know and trust;

◆ Check the *About Us* section on the web page for more information about the creator and organisation;

◆ Use another source, if possible, to check any information of which you are unsure – find two or more credible sources that say the same thing;

◆ Note whether the information has been provided to promote the sale of a product;

◆ You should check the national source of the data as information may differ between countries, especially legal issues;

◆ Look for a corporate profile or citations to previously published work;

◆ Always keep an open mind about any information you read – what assumptions are being made? Can the author prove that the information is correct? What methods were used to generate the information?

◆ Look for clues about who might have funded the research or who is sponsoring the website. Might these organisations have a vested interest in the research or results?

HOW TO CONDUCT PRIMARY RESEARCH

Before you go on to conduct your own primary research, it is useful to distinguish between *qualitative* research and *quantitative* research.

◆ **Qualitative research** – this explores attitudes, behaviour and experiences through such methods as interviews or focus groups. It attempts to get an in-depth opinion from people taking part in the research. Attitudes, behaviour and experiences are important, so fewer people take part in the research – but the contact with these people tends to last for a lot longer.

◆ **Quantitative research** – this generates statistics through the use of a large-scale survey research, using methods such as questionnaires or structured interviews. If a market researcher has stopped you in the street or you have filled in a questionnaire which has arrived through the post, this falls under the umbrella of quantitative research. This type of research reaches many more people, but the contact with those people is much quicker than it is in qualitative research.

Research methods are the tools you use to collect your data. The five most common tools used by researchers are listed below:

◆ **Interviews** – there are several different types of interview used in research. The most common of these tend to be *unstructured*, *semi-structured* and *structured* interviews.

◆ **Focus Groups** – these may be called *discussion groups* or *group interviews*. A number of people are asked to come together in a group to discuss a certain issue led by a *moderator* or *facilitator* who introduces the topic, asks specific questions, controls digressions and stops break-away conversations.

◆ **Questionnaires** – these are used for many different types of research. There are three basic types of questionnaire – closed-ended, open-ended or a combination of both. Increasingly, the internet is being used to distribute questionnaires.

◆ **Observation** – there are two main ways in which researchers observe – direct observation and participant observation (where the researcher immerses themselves into the culture of the people who are being studied).

◆ **Experimentation** – this is a popular research method used in the sciences such as chemistry and physics.

To find out how to use these different research methods, consult *A Practical Guide to Research Methods* (details below).

BEGINNING A RESEARCH PROJECT

When you start to think about your research project, a useful way of remembering the important questions to ask is to think of the five W's:

WHAT? WHY? WHO? WHERE? WHEN?

Once you have thought about these five W's you can move on to think about HOW you are going to collect your data.

WHAT?

What is your research? This question needs to be answered as specifically as possible. One of the hardest parts in the early stages of research is to be able to define your project. So much research fails because the researcher has been unable to do this. A useful tip is to sum up, in one sentence only, your research. If you are unable to do this, the chances are your research topic is too broad, ill-thought out or too obscure.

WHY?

Why do you want to do the research? What is its purpose? Think very carefully about why you are doing the research as this will affect your topic, the way you conduct the research and the way in which you report the results. If you're researching for a university dissertation or project, does your proposed research provide the opportunity to reach the required intellectual standard? Will your research generate enough material to write a dissertation of the required length? Or will your research generate too much data that would be impossible to summarise into a report of the required length?

WHO?

Who will be your participants? What type of people do you need to get in touch with and how will you contact them? If you have to conduct your research within a particular time scale, there's little point choosing a topic which would include people who are difficult or expensive to contact. Also, bear in mind that the internet now provides opportunities for contacting people cheaply.

WHERE?

Where are you going to conduct your research? Thinking about this question in geographical terms will help you to refine your research topic. The venue is also important – where would be convenient to carry out your interviews or focus groups? Is there a room at your institution which would be free of charge, or are you going to conduct them in participants' own homes? Would it be safe for you to do so? Would you be comfortable doing so? If you've answered 'no' to either of these last two questions, maybe you need to think again about your research topic.

WHEN?

When are you going to do your research? Thinking about this question will help you to sort out whether the research project you have proposed is possible within your time scale. It will also help you to think more about your participants – when you need to contact them and whether they will be available at that time.

Once you have thought about these five W's, try to sum up your proposed project in one sentence. When you have done this, take it to several people, including your tutor, and ask them if it makes sense. Do they understand what your research is about? If they don't, ask them to explain their confusion, revise your statement and take it back to them.

KEEPING RECORDS OF BACKGROUND RESEARCH

When you begin any type of background research, keep accurate records of the data you have gathered from a particular source – this will save you plenty of time and frustration later, especially when you come to write an assignment or start a research project. A useful way to organise your background research is to have two files – one for primary research and one for secondary research. Each file can be divided into topics with the relevant notes slotted into each.

For the primary research file, notes from each contact can be separated by a contact sheet which gives the name of the person, the date and time you met and a contact number or address. In the secondary research file, each page of notes can be headed by details of the publication in the same format that will be used in the bibliography (see Chapter 11).

SUMMARY

This chapter has offered advice on how to conduct primary and secondary research. Most students will be required to conduct secondary research, which typically involves using libraries and the internet, before they are required to conduct primary research. This chapter has provided an introduction to the different types of research method, along with advice on beginning a project. It is not possible to cover all aspects of the research process within this book. However, details of further reading are provided below for those students who wish to develop their research skills.

To be successful in your studies, especially when writing assignments and conducting research, you need to develop your analytical skills. These issues are discussed in the next chapter.

FURTHER READING

I have written a book for people who are new to research which covers all the areas mentioned above in much more depth. It explains clearly and concisely how to go about conducting a research project.

As your course progresses you might find it to be a useful resource, especially if you are expected to undertake a large research project or dissertation.

Dawson C. (2006) *A Practical Guide to Research Methods: A User-Friendly Guide to Mastering Research Techniques and Projects*, 2nd edition. Oxford: How to Books Ltd. (£9.99).

Developing your Analytical Skills

Developing your analytical skills is an important part of the learning process. However, in my research I have found that this is an area of study that greatly concerns adult students. This tends to be because adults feel that they do not have the required level of skill or intelligence to develop skills of reflection, analysis, synthesis and evaluation.

Over your lifetime you have already developed these skills – you may, however, be unaware of these skills or have not thought of putting a specific name to them. This chapter gives advice on cultivating analytical skills and applying them to your studies.

LEARNING HOW TO QUESTION

Everybody knows how to question. It is part of what makes us human – we meet new people and ask them where they come from, what they do for a job, whether they are married. However, as your studies progress you will find that you need to think more deeply about how you question and the type of questions that you ask.

Being able to ask the right questions is fundamental to your studies, not just when you conduct your own piece of research, but when you listen to lectures, read books and talk to other students. If you do not develop questions you will not be able to reflect on what you are learning, query the arguments of others or develop your own ideas.

Start to take notice of the questions that your tutor asks. What are the questions designed to do? What happens when a question is asked? Do some questions work better than others? Why might this be?

Questions that should be avoided include:

◆ Trick questions;

◆ Sterile questions that constrain thought;

◆ Questions that are too simple, irrelevant or patronising;

◆ Questions for which the answer is readily available;

◆ Closed questions that require only one word answers.

Questions that should be used include:

◆ Open questions that require more than one-word answers;

◆ Questions that make you think;

◆ Questions that stimulate reflection;

◆ Relevant and 'real' questions that have meaning;

◆ Questions that introduce a problem;

◆ Questions that test existing assumptions.

Take note of the questions you ask when you reflect on your work, analyse the thoughts of others, solve problems and evaluate your learning. You might find it useful to write the questions down in your learning diary as this will be a useful list to reference over the duration of your course.

CRITIQUING AND REVIEWING

On some courses you will be required to critique and review the work of others. Some adults feel uncomfortable with this, believing they are 'not clever enough' or 'too inexperienced' to do this. However, this is not the case – from a very early age we learn how to critique and review, especially from books, television and newspapers or magazines.

Critiquing and reviewing the academic work of others is similar to this – we read the text, think about what we have read, ask questions and then form our own opinions about the content. If you are concerned about carrying out your own critique, break down the task into a series of steps which will help you to make the task seem more manageable, as illustrated below:

◆ **Step 1** – Read quickly through the text to get a general idea of the content.

◆ **Step 2** – Check the meaning of any unfamiliar words or phrases.

◆ **Step 3** – Jot down a few notes about what you think the author is trying to say.

◆ **Step 4** – Jot down any questions that have formed in your mind as a result of this preliminary reading.

◆ **Step 5** – Return to the text and read it more slowly, asking yourself, what is the author trying to prove? A good author will hint at this in the introduction and summarise the point in the conclusion.

◆ **Step 6** – When you have discovered the main point (or points) the author is making, jot it down.

◆ **Step 7** – Think about this point (or thesis). Has the author backed up the point with evidence? Is this evidence adequate? Is it convincing? Are *you* convinced by what you are reading?

◆ **Step 8** – Think about the purpose of the text. Why has the author published the work? At what audience is the paper aimed? Are assumptions made within the paper about previous knowledge?

◆ **Step 9** – Think about the methodology and methods. What methods did the author use to develop this thesis? Are the methods and methodology sound and appropriate to the topic? Can you think of any problems or an alternative method that might produce different results? Don't be afraid to say that you have spotted potential problems – academic work is built on the critical review of others.

SOLVING PROBLEMS

A problem exists when you are curious, puzzled, confused or not sure how to resolve an issue. Throughout your course you should encounter a series of these types of problems that have to be solved. You will find the task easier if you consider the following points:

◆ Think about alternative ways to describe the problem.

◆ View the problem from various perspectives.

◆ Try to explain the problem to someone else.

◆ Compare different accounts or explanations of the same problem.

◆ Break the problem down into manageable parts. Omit irrelevant information.

◆ Try to supply alternatives or different outcomes.

◆ Try role play or role reversal if appropriate to the problem.

◆ Recognise important questions to ask about the problem.

◆ Ask 'What if . . . ?'

◆ Consider the consequences.

BECOMING A REFLECTIVE LEARNER

Reflective thought involves the ability to acquire facts, understand ideas and arguments, apply methodological principles, analyse and evaluate information and produce conclusions. It includes the ability to question and solve problems by linking your previous ideas, knowledge and experiences with present ideas, knowledge and experiences.

Becoming a reflective learner is a skill that is cultivated over time – you will get better as your course progresses. The following points will help you to think more about how to become a reflective learner:

◆ Your ability to reflect increases as you create mental challenges for yourself.

◆ Social interaction aids reflection.

◆ Reflection becomes easier the more you know about a topic.

◆ Your ability to reflect is increased by surrounding yourself with others who are engaged in reflection, such as fellow students and tutors.

◆ Reflection is more effective if carried out in an appropriate environment free from distraction.

◆ Constructive feedback helps your ability to reflect.

◆ Writing down your ideas helps. However, you should make sure that your writing is not purely descriptive. Instead it should include personal judgement, personal discourse and possibly an analysis of outside influences on your thought processes.

Reflection takes place at different speeds, levels and intensities. When you are first presented with an idea you may find that you rapidly reflect on what is being said. After the speaker has finished you might rapidly evaluate, forming your own ideas. Later you might think about the ideas in more depth, slowly, taking your time. Then you might return to the idea at a later date, when something else reminds you of what you have learned. At this time you are able to bring in new ideas that help to build upon what you have learned previously.

HYPOTHESISING AND THEORISING

In the 'traditional' science view, a hypothesis is an idea about a phenomenon or observation that is put forward for testing. At this stage it is tentative and not proven. However, once it has been tested repeatedly and the probability of error has been greatly reduced, the hypothesis can be developed into a theory. For a theory to stand up to scientific scrutiny, evidence for its development must be shown clearly and it must be able to explain existing phenomena and make predictions about the future.

In this view there are four main stages that you would need to work through to develop your theory:

1) Ask questions in the form of a hypothesis.
2) Look for patterns to support or disprove your hypothesis.
3) Formulate your theory, based on the hypothesis.
4) Design experiments to test your theory.

This type of theory generation is *deductive*, that is, the theory has been deduced from the hypothesis which was developed and then tested by the scientist. However, there is another type of theory generation which uses an *inductive* method.

Procedures for this type of theory generation may vary depending upon the methodological standpoint of the researcher, but in general you would need to work through the following stages:

1) Begin your enquiry by observing a phenomenon or behaviour.
2) Develop your research questions based on these observations.
3) Answer these questions through more in-depth observation or questioning.
4) Develop your theory, based on these in-depth observations.
5) Test and modify your theory with further observation.

The nature, development, importance and use of hypotheses and theories is questioned and challenged by some academics. In particular, the overriding importance of logic and strict mathematical form is contested by some philosophers and social scientists. If this subject interests you, further reading is suggested at the end of this chapter.

RECOGNISING OBJECTIVITY AND SUBJECTIVITY
In scientific terms objectivity is taken to mean knowledge or theory which is free from bias. To achieve this it must have passed rigorous tests for validity and reliability. There are many tests that purport to do this and scientists must follow strict rules if they are to have their work taken seriously by the scientific community. If you are engaged in this type of scientific research you will need to enrol on a suitable research module to help you to develop these skills.

Subjectivity is often described as being 'of a person' – everything that makes us who we are influences our knowledge and theory generation. This may include our background, our likes and dislikes, the society and culture in which we live and the time in history in which we are working and studying.

As your studies progress it is important to have an awareness of objectivity and subjectivity. It will help you to analyse and make judgements about what you are reading and it will help you when you come to do your own research. However, try not to follow the line of thought that suggests that objectivity is good and subjectivity is bad. There are some fantastic pieces of research that have been conducted in a highly subjective manner – indeed, some people would argue that true objectivity is impossible to obtain.

SUMMARY

For your studies to be successful it is important to cultivate your skills of analysis. This includes your ability to ask questions, critique and review the work of others, solve problems, reflect on your learning, hypothesise and theorise and recognise objectivity and subjectivity. This chapter has provided advice on how to go about enhancing your skills of analysis. Although adult students are sometimes concerned that they do not have the ability to develop these skills, it is often adults who develop and display these skills the most in their research and writing.

Another area of concern for adult students is the oral presentation. The next chapter provides advice and guidance on preparing and giving an oral presentation.

FURTHER READING

If any of the issues discussed in this chapter interest you, the following books cover the subject in much more depth:

Calhoun, C. (1995) *Critical Social Theory*, Cambridge, MA: Blackwell.

Harding, S. (1991) *Whose Science? Whose Knowledge? Thinking From Women's Lives*, Buckingham: Open University Press.

Layder, D. (1994) *Understanding Social Theory*, London: Sage.

(14)

Conquering Oral Presentations

During some research with adult learners, I found that the part of the course that filled them with the most dread, after examinations, was the oral presentation. However, once a session had been arranged to discuss their fears and anxieties, and they had been given the opportunity to practise within a supportive environment, adults felt much more at ease about making a presentation.

The number, type and level of oral presentation that is required will depend upon your course. On many under-graduate courses you will be required to conduct a seminar in which the purpose is for you to present a topic and then encourage questions and opinions from other members of the seminar group. On other courses you may be required to make a group presentation on a piece of group work. Other students may be required to make an oral presentation on their research findings. This chapter provides advice and guidance suitable for all types of oral presentation required at college or university.

PRESENTING A SEMINAR

The secret to presenting a good seminar is preparation. Thorough preparation will help you to control your nerves and you will feel much more relaxed and confident about your ability. If you know your subject well and show an interest, you will also come across to others in the group as professional and knowledgeable. They will be happy to listen to what you have to say and will be willing to participate in the discussion.

You can begin your background preparation as soon as you start to attend seminars – these will show you what goes well and what goes badly within a seminar environment. Listen to the presenters and watch what they do – how do they speak? What does their body language say? Do they vary their pitch and tone? What hand and facial gestures do they use? How do they present their information? Is the information easy to understand or muddled and confused? Do they hold your attention? If not, why not? What visual aids do they use? Are they effective? Is there anything you think that the presenter could do better?

Through observing seminars in this way, you will begin to get a clearer idea of what works well and what you should avoid. You can then go on to prepare your own seminar. The following points will help in this preparation:

◆ Begin your preparation at least two weeks before the date of your seminar. This will give you a chance to read around the subject and follow up any points that need clarification.

◆ Make sure that you understand the topic you have to discuss. If in doubt, seek advice from your tutor.

◆ Think about what handouts you are going to give to the seminar group. It can be useful to hand out a copy of your seminar paper. This outlines all your ideas and arguments on the topic in a structured way, similar to an essay. Producing this type of seminar paper will help you to think logically about the topic and put your ideas onto paper in a coherent way. Some tutors will require you to produce a seminar paper which you must hand in as part of your assessed work.

◆ Think about what visual aids you are going to use. By now you should have some experience of what works well in a seminar setting – perhaps another student produced a PowerPoint presentation that worked well, or another used an overhead projector (OHP) effectively (see below). Keep in mind what visual aids you intend to use as you write your paper. This will help you to note key points or arguments that could be included on OHP transparencies or PowerPoint templates.

◆ Tackle your seminar paper as you would a written assignment:
  ◆ identify key areas
  ◆ begin reading
  ◆ take notes
  ◆ develop arguments
  ◆ write a draft
  ◆ rewrite
  ◆ return to the reading if necessary
  ◆ edit and proofread.

◆ Produce your visual aids. When you present a seminar you should not read straight from your paper. This is an ineffective method of presentation that can be boring for other members of the seminar group. You need to produce visual aids that will help you to speak around the topic. They will serve to aid your memory and give others something to look at while you speak.

◆ Produce a list of questions that you can ask to stimulate discussion.

◆ Practise your talk. Time yourself to check that it lasts for roughly the right amount of time. You may find it useful to practice in front of a friend or to record yourself – this will help you to analyse your style of presentation.

Before the seminar takes place make sure that you have with you all your handouts, your visual aids and anything else you may require. Turn up early so that you can rearrange furniture if required and set up and test any equipment you will be using.

During the seminar speak clearly and confidently, slowing your speech and lowering your voice tone very slightly. This will help you to control any voice 'wobbles' caused by nervousness. The list of *do's* and *don'ts* below will help you to think further about your presentation technique.

USING VISUAL AIDS

Your audience will find your presentation more interesting if you use visual aids. However, whichever visual aid you decide to use must be used with care – poor visual aids can detract from what you are saying and distract the attention of your audience.

You must check that all equipment is available and working for your seminar. It is advisable to have a contingency or back-up plan should anything not work on the day.

Overhead Projectors

You can photocopy key points onto transparencies that can be used with overhead projectors (OHPs). Only include a few lines of words or diagrams on each page and make sure that the font size is not too small, otherwise your audience will be unable to read what you have written. Keywords, diagrams or phrases should be used to aid your talk – you will find that one transparency should last for about three minutes of your presentation. If you intend to use an OHP, practise beforehand so that you know how to use it and which way up the transparencies should be presented. Check that the equipment is working properly before the presentation.

PowerPoint

PowerPoint is a useful presentation graphics program which enables you to create slides that can be shared live or online. You can enhance your presentation with animation, artwork and diagrams which make it more interesting for your audience. However, you should not rely on PC presentations and should always have some form of back-up, such as OHP transparencies in case of equipment failure on the day. Full details about PowerPoint can be found at www.microsoft.com/office/powerpoint.

Handouts

It is useful to let your audience take away something from your presentation so that they can remember what you have said at a later date. However, be careful when you give out pieces of paper – people might read them straightaway instead of listening to what you have to say. For most presentations it is best to give handouts at the end of your speech. Always include your name, contact e-mail and the title of your paper on any handouts. If you are making a presentation to an outside organisation, also include your college or university.

White/Black Board or Flip Chart

You may prefer to write down key points as your presentation progresses, especially if you are inviting contributions from other members of the group. If you are intending to use this method, make sure that you have a suitable pen or chalk of your own because you cannot guarantee that there will be any available in the room. Be careful not to buy a permanent marker pen if you are using a wipe clean board. You will also need to check that there is enough paper available on a flip chart. If you intend to use this method, write as clearly as possible, stand to the side of the board or chart and make sure that you are confident in spelling any technical terms.

DO'S AND DON'TS OF MAKING A PRESENTATION

Do:

◆ Arrive early and make sure the room is set out in the way that you want. Make sure that all the equipment is available and that you know how to work it.

- ◆ Try to relax and breathe deeply. If it is your first presentation, acknowledge the fact and remember that people will tend to help you along.

- ◆ Produce aide memoirs, either on cards, paper, OHP transparencies or presentation software such as Power-Point.

- ◆ Make it clear from the outset whether you are happy to be interrupted or whether questions should be left until the end. If you have invited questions, make sure that you make every effort to answer them.

- ◆ Look around the room while you are speaking – if it's a small group, make eye contact with as many people as possible.

- ◆ Present interesting visual information such as graphs, charts and tables in a format which can be viewed by everyone.

- ◆ Alter the tone and pitch of your voice, length of sentence and facial/hand gestures to maintain the interest of your audience. Show that you are interested in your subject.

- ◆ Define carefully all technical terms.

- ◆ Produce a paper or handout which people can take away with them.

- ◆ Talk to people after your presentation and ask them how it went and whether there are any improvements that they might suggest for future presentations.

Don't

◆ Rush in late, find that the overhead projector doesn't work and that you have no pen for the whiteboard.

◆ Worry about showing your nerves. Everybody gets nervous when they first start giving presentations and your audience should know this.

◆ Read straight from a paper you have written.

◆ Bluff your way through and hope people won't notice.

◆ Apologise, giggle, fiddle, scratch or sniff.

◆ Get cross if you are interrupted and have not mentioned that you don't want this to happen.

◆ Invite questions and then not answer them or patronise the inquirer.

◆ Produce visual information which people can't see, either due to its size or print quality.

◆ Present in a monotone voice with no facial/hand gestures.

◆ Make it clear that your subject bores the pants off you.

◆ Run over time unless everyone is happy to do so.

◆ Let the audience go home without any record of what you have said.

◆ Run away never to be seen again.

OVERCOMING NERVES

Remember that even the most experienced of presenters still get nervous when they make speeches. Often it is that extra amount of adrenalin produced that gets you through the presentation and makes it much more interesting and animated that it would be otherwise. Most of the other students in your group will need to make their own presentations and will be nervous. This helps you as they will be willing you to do well, just as you will be willing them to do well.

The following points will help you to control your nerves when making a presentation:

◆ Learn breathing techniques. When you breathe fully and deeply from your stomach you automatically slow your breath which helps to control nerves and tension.

◆ Talk about your concerns and worries with other students. Ask your tutor to discuss making presentations in class.

◆ Know your subject and practise your speech. It will help you to feel more confident.

◆ Speak to people as they arrive. It will help you to get used to the sound of your own voice.

◆ Ask a friend to sit in your line of vision. They will be able to offer encouragement from the audience.

◆ Have water available during your presentation. This will help if your mouth dries or your throat begins to tickle.

Making a Presentation – Student Tips

I nearly became a nervous wreck worrying about my first seminar. I won't lie and say it was easy, but it was much better than I expected. I had wasted a lot of time worrying about what might happen when nothing bad happened at all. My tip would be to prepare really well, get down to the nitty gritty and not worry about how it will go. If you know enough, it'll be fine. Everybody knows you're nervous – they're all the same, so they tend to help you through as much as possible. **(Janine, 37)**

Don't hold pieces of paper 'cos if you're nervous they will shake madly. I found it useful to write my key points on bits of card which didn't shake when my hands shook. **(Brenda, 43)**

Don't try and make jokes unless you're a born comedian. I tried and they fell so flat it was ridiculous. Apparently, a seminar isn't the place for bad jokes! **(Bob, 52)**

Have you heard that one about thinking of your audience as naked? Well it didn't work for me, but I thought of them as school children instead, and I had to help them because they were more nervous and less knowledgeable than me. It really calmed me down and stopped me thinking that everyone would ask questions that I just couldn't answer. **(June, 29)**

Be confident and be assertive. Show you know what you're talking about and people will believe you! **(Anne, 29)**

Ask people if you have a phrase that you use a lot. If you do, become aware of when you use that phrase and begin to stop yourself using it so much. It will stop people in your seminar becoming distracted by counting how many times you say 'to be fair', or 'in other words'. **(Martha, 58)**

Persuade your tutor to let you do your first presentation in a group – you get support from everyone and you can share the tasks. **(Ian, 22)**

◆ Slow down your speech and pitch your voice at a lower level. You are less likely to squeak or cough if you do this.

◆ Don't fear your audience – most, if not all, will be willing you to succeed.

SUMMARY

Although many adult students are nervous about having to make a presentation, there are several things that you can do to help ease your nerves and to help your presentation to run smoothly. These include observing others, preparing carefully and using appropriate visual aids. It is also important to be aware of body language, facial movements, pitch and tone of voice. Many adults find that once they have completed their first presentation the process becomes a lot easier. Many also point out that they had worried unnecessarily and that their presentation ran much more smoothly than they had expected.

On undergraduate courses you may be required to run seminars every year. In your final year you will also be required to produce a dissertation, which is an extended piece of research that will count towards your final marks. Advice on completing your dissertation is provided in the next chapter.

15

Completing your Dissertation

Most higher education students, in the third year of their course, will be required to complete a dissertation. This is a piece of research or a long project which has to be written up into a report that counts towards your final marks. The length of your dissertation will vary between course and institution, but in general it will be between 8,000 and 20,000 words.

A report of such length may seem incredibly daunting, especially if you are just beginning your course. However, by your third year you will have developed your research and writing skills to an extent that will make writing your dissertation easier and more enjoyable. This chapter provides advice on completing your dissertation.

CHOOSING A TOPIC

Your dissertation is an independent piece of research on which you decide the topic. By the time you have reached your third year you will have gained a good idea of the topics within your subject that interest you. As your third year progresses, keep a list of all the areas on your course that fascinate you – remember to add to the list any ideas or thoughts about your area of interest. This list will provide a useful resource when you come to choose your dissertation topic.

When choosing a topic, you should bear in mind the following points:

◆ Don't leave decisions until the last minute – start to think about possible topics early in your third year.

◆ Choose something in which you are interested – it will help you to keep motivated.

◆ Try to narrow down your topic – you will find that a general area is much harder to research and it is difficult to focus your reading. You will be able to find plenty of information for the narrowest of topics.

◆ When you have made a choice, sum up your topic in one sentence. This will help you to focus on what you intend to do, and will help you to decide whether you have clearly defined your intended project.

◆ Once you have made a choice speak to your tutor as soon as possible. They will be able to tell you whether the topic is acceptable for your course and whether you have chosen something that is feasible to research in the allotted time. Don't waste time beginning background research on a topic that will not be suitable.

◆ Once you have chosen a topic and it has been passed by your tutor, try not to change your mind. Persevere with the background reading, even if it seems daunting and confusing at first. If you are really struggling, seek extra guidance from your tutor.

◆ Don't waste time thinking too much about a title at this stage – this will become clearer as your work progresses. However, try to produce a working title which you can change as you proceed. This will help you to keep focused.

CHOOSING YOUR RESEARCH METHODS

Research methods are the tools you use to collect your data (see Chapter 12). Before you choose the most appropriate methods for your research, you will need to familiarise yourself with the various methods available. Your library will contain many research methods books, but it is advisable to begin first with a general introduction to research methods. This is because many of the books can be complicated and full of technical jargon which can be confusing to you if you are new to research. You may find another of my books, *A Practical Guide to Research Methods*, helpful as it assumes no prior knowledge and is written in a user-friendly way (see Chapter 12).

PLANNING AND PREPARATION

For most dissertations you will need to produce a *research proposal*. This is a document which sets out your ideas in an easily accessible way. Even if you have not been asked specifically to produce a research proposal by your tutor, it is a good idea to do so – it helps you to focus your ideas and provides a useful document for you to reference, should your research wander off track a little.

All research proposals should contain the following information:

◆ **Title** – this should be short and explanatory. At this stage it only needs to be a working title.

◆ **Background** – this section should contain a rationale for your research. Why have you chosen this topic? Why is the research needed? This rationale should be placed within the context of existing research or within your own experience and/or observation. You need to demonstrate that you know what you're talking about and that you have knowledge of the literature surrounding this topic, so you will need to conduct preliminary background research before you write your proposal. If you're unable to find any other research which deals specifically with your proposed project, you need to say so, illustrating how your proposed research will fill this gap. If there is other work which has covered this area, you need to show how your work will build on and add to the existing knowledge.

◆ **Aims and Objectives** – the aim is the overall driving force of the research and the objectives are the means by which you intend to achieve the aims. These must be clear and succinct. Some tutors, however, will ask only for one or two aims and may not require objectives.

◆ **Research Methods** – in this section you need to describe your proposed research methods and justify their use. Why have you decided to use those particular methods? Why are other methods not appropriate? This section might need to include details about samples, numbers of people to be contacted, method of data collection, methods of data analysis and ethical considerations.

◆ **Timetable** – a detailed timetable scheduling all aspects of the research for your dissertation should be produced. This may need to include the time taken to conduct background research, questionnaire or interview schedule development, data collection, data analysis and report writing. Conducting research almost always takes longer than you anticipate. Allow for this and add a few extra weeks on to each section of your timetable. Make sure that you start your dissertation early enough to cover yourself if you do need extra time.

◆ **Budget and Resources** – check that you need this section – some tutors will want to know that you have thought carefully about what resources are needed and from where you expect to obtain these. Some types of research are more expensive than others and if you're on a limited budget you will have to think about this when making a decision.

◆ **Dissemination** – what do you expect to do with the results of your research? How are you going to let people know about what you have found out? Generally, it will suffice to say that the results will be produced in an undergraduate dissertation which will be made available in the university library.

DOING YOUR RESEARCH

Conducting the research for your dissertation may be the first piece of autonomous research you have had to undertake for your course. You will find the process a little easier if you bear in mind the following points:

◆ Do not procrastinate (see Chapter 3). Begin your research as soon as possible and adhere to your time-table.

◆ If you are using a particular method, such as a questionnaire or an interview, practise first. This is called *piloting* and is extremely important because it will save you wasting your time on a method that may not be gathering the data you require.

◆ Ask the participants of your pilot survey to say what they think about your questionnaire or your interview technique. They may have found some of the questions confusing and you may need to alter them.

◆ Analyse the data from your pilot survey to see if it is yielding the type of information you require. If not, revise your methods.

◆ Keep a research diary as your work progresses. This will be useful when you come to write the research methods section of your dissertation. Pay attention to what goes well and what goes badly. Have you had to revise your methods? Why? This is not an admission of failure but instead shows that you are able to evaluate and critique your methods. No research methods are perfect.

◆ Think carefully about how you are going to organise and file your data. Do you have somewhere safe and secure? What are you going to do about backing up the data?

◆ Utilise all the help available at your university – ask for advice about data analysis at the computing centre, enrol on a research methods short course and make good use of your tutor.

WRITING YOUR DISSERTATION

Speak to your tutor before you begin writing to find out whether the rules of your university require you to produce your dissertation in a specific format. If not, the generally accepted structure is as follows:

Title Page

This contains the title of the dissertation, the name of the student and the date of completion. It will include details about the purpose of the dissertation, for example: 'A dissertation submitted in partial fulfilment of the requirements of Kent University for the degree of BA Honours Combined Humanities'.

Contents Page

This section lists the contents of the report, either in chapter or section headings with sub-headings, and their page numbers.

List of Illustrations

This section includes title and page number of all graphs, tables, illustrations, charts, etc.

Acknowledgements

Some researchers may wish to acknowledge the help of their research participants, tutors, employers and/or funding body.

Abstract/Summary

This tends to be a one page summary of the research, its purpose, methods, main findings and conclusion.

Introduction

This section introduces the research, setting out the aims and objectives, terms and definitions. It includes a rationale for the research and a summary of the dissertation structure.

Background

This section includes all your background research, which may be obtained from the literature, from personal experience or both. You must indicate the source of all your references, so remember to keep a complete record of everything you read.

Research Methods

This section sets out a description of, and justification for, the chosen research methods. Remember to include all the practical information examiners will need to evaluate your work – for example, how many people took part, how they were chosen, your time scale and data recording and analysis methods. If something did not work well, say why this happened and what action you took to address the problem. Examiners will not take this as failure but will see that you are able to critique your methods and address the problems you have encountered. Don't try to cover up if things have gone wrong – most examiners will spot this action.

Findings/Analysis

This section includes your main findings. The content of this section will depend on your chosen methodology and methods. If you have conducted a large quantitative survey, this section may contain tables, graphs, pie charts and associated statistics. If you have conducted a qualitative piece of research this section may consist of descriptive prose containing lengthy quotations.

Conclusion

This section sums up your findings and draws conclusions from them, perhaps in relation to other research or literature.

Further Research

How could your research be continued? Perhaps some results are inconclusive or perhaps the research has thrown up many more research questions which could be addressed? It is useful to include this section because it shows that you are aware of the wider picture and that you are not trying to cover up something which you feel may be lacking from your own work.

References

This section includes all the literature to which you have referred in your report.

Bibliography

If you have read other books in relation to your research but not actually referred to them when writing up your report, you should include them in a bibliography. However, make sure that they are still relevant to your work.

Appendices

If you have constructed a questionnaire for your research, or produced an interview schedule or a code of ethics, it may be useful to include this in your report as an appendix. In general, appendices do not count towards your total amount of words so it is a useful way of including material without taking up space that can be used for other information. However, do not attempt to fill up your report with irrelevant appendices as this will not impress examiners. When including material you must make sure that it is relevant – ask yourself whether the examiner will gain a deeper understanding of your work by reading the appendix, and if not, leave it out.

WHAT MAKES A GOOD DISSERTATION?

◆ The topic is relevant to your course.

◆ The research is unique or offers new insight or development.

◆ The title, aims and objectives are all clear and succinct.

◆ You have conducted some thorough and comprehensive background research which is well referenced.

◆ You have chosen suitable research methods and used them well – you are able to critique them if something didn't work as planned.

◆ The report is the right length, well-written, well-structured, well-presented and free from mistakes.

◆ Your arguments are convincing and well thought-out.

◆ Your conclusion is interesting and provides a good summary of the research.

WHAT MAKES A BAD DISSERTATION?

◆ Your aims and objectives are unclear or vague, or you don't meet them when you do your research and write the report.

◆ Your research methods are unsuitable for the topic and do not produce the required results.

◆ The overall plan is too ambitious and difficult to achieve in the timescale.

◆ You have not conducted enough in-depth background research.

◆ Information about the data collection is lacking or not detailed enough.

◆ Your research and report are pitched at the wrong level.

◆ You have jumped to inappropriate conclusions that are not backed up with evidence.

◆ The work is not completed on time.

◆ Your dissertation is poorly presented with spelling mistakes, grammatical errors and problems with style, structure and content.

Completing your Dissertation – Student Tips

Meet with your tutor straightaway. You need to know that you will get on with him or her and that they will be able to help you. If you don't like your tutor find out if you can change, but do it early. **(Stephen, 24)**

I found it useful to hand in a draft chapter quite early to my tutor. She told me where I was going wrong so I could put it right before I'd written too much else. **(Kate, 33)**

In my second year I decided one of the modules I would study would be research methods. That way it saved me no end of time in background reading when I came to do my dissertation, and I didn't have to spend too much time deciding which methods I would use. **(Anne, 29)**

Look at other dissertations before you start. It gives you an idea of what is required. But ask your tutor which are good ones and which are not so good before you do this. **(Mark, 41)**

Get a list of the university rules and regulations as soon as possible. I was surprised to see some quite strict guidelines about what you can and can't do for your dissertation, especially in terms of how it has to be laid out. **(Jamie, 22)**

Ignore what other students are doing – don't try and compete, just get on with your own work in your own good time. **(Wendy, 32)**

SUMMARY

Many adult students find that, by their third year, they are looking forward to completing a dissertation. This is because it provides the opportunity to concentrate on a piece of work in which they have a high level of interest and it enables them to work in their own time using their own initiative. However, if you find the task a little daunting, there are several things you can do to make the process easier. This includes holding full preparatory meetings with your tutor and conducting thorough background research so that you become familiar with your subject and the research methods you intend to use. This chapter has provided advice on preparing for and writing your dissertation.

In addition to writing your dissertation in the third year, you will probably be required to conduct your final year exams. This tends to be the part of the course that fills adult students with the most dread. Advice for coping with examinations is provided in the next chapter.

(16)

Passing your Exams

During some of my research with adult learners it was found that one of the factors discouraging people from returning to education was the fear of taking examinations. Some of the participants felt that, as adults, they would find it hard to remember and retain the information they had learned during their course.

Many adult educators believe that examinations are not the most appropriate way to test an adult's knowledge and understanding, preferring instead to choose other methods of assessment. If you have not yet chosen a course, and examinations fill you with dread, consider choosing a course that is not examined – there are plenty to choose from.

If, however, you are already enrolled on a course with examinations, you should not become anxious – there are many things that you can do to increase your chances of success. These issues are discussed in this chapter.

HOW TO REVISE
Revision should not be an activity carried out only prior to examinations. Instead, you should aim to regularly revise your coursework throughout the year. If you do this you will

find that the information is easier to retain when it comes to examination time. If you try to 'cram' in your revision in the few weeks leading up to your exams you will probably find it stressful and less effective than methodical and sustained study carried out throughout your course.

Depending on the nature and structure of your course, you may find that it is best to spend some time revising after each topic has been completed, or you may find it easier to revise during holidays or reading breaks – half term, Christmas, Easter and summer vacations.

Whenever you decide to carry out your revision, remember to revise only topics that have been covered on your course – you should not be asked about issues other than these during the exams.

The following steps will help you to organise your revision:

◆ **Step 1 – Review and revise topics**. As each topic is completed, read through your lecture and seminar notes, noting down key words and ideas that have been raised. Some people find it useful to do this in the margins of their lecture notes, whereas others find it more effective to write these on cards which they then file under specific topics.

◆ **Step 2 – Obtain copies of previous exam papers**. Ask your tutor to supply you with some copies of previous examination papers, or obtain these from the library or college intranet. Some students prefer to do this before they start their revision because it gives them an idea of the standard that is required. If you are unsure of anything at this stage, go to your course tutor or personal tutor to discuss any issues of concern. Most tutors will run a session on examinations and what is expected of you nearer to the exam date. Remember that the course syllabus may have changed over the years, so don't panic if a different topic appears on a previous exam paper.

◆ **Step 3 – Construct a revision timetable**. The amount of time that you spend on your revision will depend upon your personal learning style, your course and the type and number of exams you are required to complete. Most students begin their main revision around 6–10 weeks before their exams are due to start. The best advice is to start earlier than you think you should – that way you can take your time to revise rather than become agitated that time is running out. If you find that you have started too early you can take a valuable and well-earned rest. When you construct your revision timetable, remember to include breaks, family commitments and anything else that takes up your time. Fill in the dates of examinations in red pen or highlight them so that you are completely sure of the date and time of each examination.

◆ **Step 4 – Consult your course syllabus**. Check that you have material for all the areas included in your syllabus – you could be asked questions on any of these topics. However, do not waste time revising any topic that is not listed in your course syllabus.

◆ **Step 5 – Break each topic into key areas**. Use your previous lecture notes and background revision to create a list of the key areas within each topic. Read over your notes again.

◆ **Step 6 – Think of questions that could be asked**. Look at the key areas within each topic and try to think of questions that could be asked about each of these areas. Try answering the questions in outline form. If you find that you have some information missing, return to your notes or find relevant information from your library. However, be careful with background reading at this stage – use it only to fill in any missing gaps – don't be tempted to start reading new information, however interesting it may appear.

◆ **Step 7 – Choose favourite key areas**. Within each topic choose two or three of your favourite areas to study in more depth. These are the areas on which you will hope to answer a question, and if you think about these well in advance, it helps you to feel more comfortable and confident in the exam. These could be issues on which you have already written an assignment, or they could be areas that interest you. You could consult previous exam papers to see what type of questions have been asked on these areas in the past. Think of your own questions and try answering them in outline form. Again, return to your reading if you feel any information is missing.

◆ **Step 8 – Draw up a summary of key facts**. On some courses you will need to remember certain facts or figures. If this is the case with your course, produce a sheet of the information you have to remember and spend some time committing it to memory. Many exams, however, are designed to test your knowledge and understanding, not your memory, so don't spend too much time trying to remember endless facts and figures.

◆ **Step 9 – Try answering a previous question under mock conditions**. Some tutors can arrange for you to do this with other students, or you can try this on your own. It is a useful exercise if you are new to exams because it helps you to know how much information you can write and how you perform within the set time.

PREPARING FOR EXAMINATIONS

Good preparation for exams will help you to control your nerves. The more prepared you are, the more relaxed you become. The following list will help with your preparation:

◆ Find out the exact date and time of your exams and make sure that you have noted this in your revision timetable. Make sure that you check the times of exams as soon as they are released because you will need to see that there are no clashes. If there are clashes you must inform your tutor or course director immediately.

◆ Find out the location of the building. Many students find it useful to visit unfamiliar venues beforehand. That way you will not be confronted with any surprises on examination day. If you have mobility problems you need to make sure that the building is accessible. Also, if you have to travel to the venue you need to find out about car-parking or the proximity of public transport.

◆ If you are entitled to extra time on medical grounds, such as dyslexia, injury or disability, make sure that you obtain a letter from your course director and take it with you to the exam. You will need to show the invigilator that you are entitled to this extra time. Make sure that you use any extra time to which you are entitled.

◆ Find out what form of identity you need to take – some will request your Students' Union card, others will request your library card. Make sure that you remember to take this with you.

◆ Speak to your tutor about what you are allowed to take into the exam. This will depend upon the rules and regulations at your college or university. For some courses you will be allowed to take in certain text books, whereas for others you will be allowed to take in a calculator or other equipment. Find out well in advance what you can take in and check with your tutor that anything you intend to take conforms to the rules.

◆ Find out which pens help you to write the quickest and which are the most comfortable to use. Buy several of these pens and make sure that you take at least two to each exam.

◆ Do not try to cram in any last minute revision the night before. Instead, try to relax and unwind – treat yourself to a stress-free evening if possible.

TAKING AN EXAMINATION

Prior to your exam try to get a good night's sleep. Check that your alarm clock is reliable and ask that someone makes sure that you have got up on time. Make sure that you arrive at the venue at least ten minutes before the exam is due to begin.

Rules and regulations vary about late arrivals – at some institutions you will be able to enter the room for up to 30 minutes after the start, but for others there will be no late entry. If you are late for any reason and are not allowed into the room, you must report to your course office or tutor immediately and explain the reason for being late. At some institutions you may be allowed to re-sit the exam.

Once in the exam hall you should follow the points listed below:

◆ Do not look at the exam paper until you are told to do so by the invigilator.

◆ When you are told to turn over the paper read all instructions carefully. Find out how many questions you are expected to answer. Note whether there are any questions that are compulsory. Find out whether you have to answer a certain number of questions from each section.

◆ Work out how much time you have for each question – your tutor will probably have told you this beforehand, but make sure it does not differ on your paper. Note the amount of marks each section is worth, if this information is supplied. Those sections with more marks will require more time to be spent on them.

◆ Read *all* the questions before you start to write your answers. As you go through them, tick any you think you could answer.

◆ Check all sides of the exam paper to make sure that you haven't missed any information.

◆ Some institutions will give you *reading time* before you go on to answer questions. Use this time wisely to make sure that you understand all that is being asked of you. Make some notes as you read the questions.

◆ Answer your best question first – this will help you to relax and the information should flow well.

◆ Write as clearly and as legibly as possible.

◆ Go on to answer the other questions – keep an eye on the time and make sure that you spend only the required time on each answer and then move on. You can always come back to an unfinished answer at the end.

◆ If you are stuck recollecting a fact or figure, leave a blank space – you may find that you remember later.

◆ If you find yourself running out of time, jot down the main points you wanted to include in the rest of the answer – some examiners will give you one or two more points for this.

◆ Once you have finished an exam, start to think about the next one. Don't spend unnecessary time and energy worrying about how you've done – it's always very hard to tell.

IMPROVING EXAMINATION MARKS

The following tips have been provided by tutors who regularly mark examination papers:

◆ Make sure that you follow the instructions carefully – you wouldn't believe how many people answer the wrong number of questions. If an answer is missing you will get no marks for that question which greatly reduces your overall mark, however good it may be.

◆ Answer all the questions – don't make the mistake of spending too much time on one and then not having enough time to start another. You will receive better marks for partial answers than no answer at all.

◆ Make sure that your information is relevant to the question – you get no extra marks for padding your answers with irrelevant material, and all you are doing is wasting your valuable time.

◆ In mathematical papers always write down the steps you take to work out a problem – you get marks for these steps, even if your answer is wrong. Do not cross out answers that you think are wrong – let the examiner decide. You will not get any marks for work that has been crossed out, even if it is right.

SUMMARY

Although many adults are worried about examinations there are many steps that you can take to reduce your stress and anxiety. These include careful organisation and revision of notes throughout the academic year, systematic revision beginning 6–10 weeks prior to exam dates, detailed preparation on the day of the exam and careful reading of instructions and questions once in the examination room. This chapter has provided advice on all these areas.

As an adult student you may find that you have more pressures on your study than younger students who do not have family and work commitments. Adults point out that the stress of examinations can add to this pressure. The next chapter provides advice and guidance on coping with the pressures of study.

17

Coping with the Pressures of Study

As adults it can be harder to cope with the pressures of study because you have so many other demands on your time. Many of you maintain full time jobs while you are studying; others raise families; some do both. Sometimes, you can be harder on yourself in terms of what you see as success and failure. You have invested so much in your studies that you are desperate to do well and prove to others that it has all been worthwhile.

These feelings create extra pressure for adults. However, there are several tactics for dealing with this added pressure, and colleges and universities provide a number of services to help students who need to talk through their problems and concerns. This chapter offers advice on coping with the pressures of study.

BUILDING RELATIONSHIPS WITH YOUR TUTOR

Although you may think of your tutor as an instructor or conveyor of knowledge, you should also think of them as a partner in the learning process. They should help you to utilise your experience and to draw out your existing knowledge. They do this through a process of questioning and by providing feedback. Any feedback your tutor gives in regards of your work should be read or listened to carefully and you should act upon their advice. Most tutors are experienced lecturers and markers – they want you to get the most out of your studies and they want you to succeed.

However, some tutors are better than others at providing 'constructive' or 'positive' feedback. Some may appear blunt or rude – don't take their comments personally, but try to read them for what they are – helpful pieces of advice on how your work can improve. If you really do feel that the comments are wrong or unjust, you can arrange to discuss them with your tutor, but you need to be aware that some tutors do not take kindly to having their comments criticised.

In some rare cases you may find that you cannot get on with your tutor. If this is the case, see if it possible to change – you will need to develop a good working relationship to get the most from their feedback.

However, most adults find that they build positive and lasting relationships with their tutors. Many tutors, especially those with experience of working with adults, are willing to discuss all issues of concern and to help students to work through their problems. If you are experiencing any sort of difficulty, you tutor may be a useful person to approach in the first instance.

COPING WITH STRESS

As we have seen above, as an adult student you will have many more demands on your time than younger students. This can lead to stressful situations that can have an adverse influence on your studies. The table below lists some of the symptoms of stress. However, some of these symptoms can be due to other medical conditions and if you are concerned about any problems you are experiencing you should always consult your doctor. Doctors at your university medical centre are experienced in the problems faced by students.

PHYSICAL	PYSCHOLOGICAL	BEHAVIOURAL
Skin rashes	Mood swings	Over and under eating
Lump in the throat	Worrying unreasonably	Working extra and long hours
Tickling cough	Excessive concern about physical health	Unreasonable complaining
Pain or tightness in chest	Constant withdrawal	Accident proneness
Palpitations	Tiredness	Poor work, cheating and evasion
Frequent indigestion	Lack of concentration	Increased dependency on drugs
Stomach pains or diarrhoea	Increased anxiety	Careless driving
Muscle tension, neck, shoulder or back pain	Increased irritability	Change in sleep patterns
Persistent headaches	Excessive daydreaming	Increased absenteeism
Double vision or difficulty focusing eyes	Inability to feel sympathy for others	Delayed recovery from accidents and illnesses

Table 5. Symptoms of stress

If you believe you are suffering from stress, remember that it is not a sign of weakness, nor is it permanent. The following tips may help you to cope:

◆ Talk about your problems and anxieties with family, friends and/or tutors.

◆ Escape from your worries for a while – take a break if at all possible.

◆ Use physical activity to help you overcome anger and frustration. Your college or university will provide a wide variety of sporting opportunities.

◆ Don't be afraid to give in or to admit that you are wrong.

◆ Be selective in your tasks – drop everything that is not essential.

◆ You don't have to be a perfectionist all the time. Consistent high marks are not the be all and end all of your course.

◆ Don't criticise yourself, or others, too much.

◆ Avoid competition. Try to cultivate co-operation instead. Gaining support from other students will help with your studies and your personal life.

◆ Allocate yourself recreation time and make sure that you use it.

◆ Learn to say no to others who are demanding too much of your time.

◆ Try to work out why you are tense and worried. Try to alter the situation that is causing the trouble.

◆ Think through stressful events before they happen. Be well prepared.

◆ Learn relaxation techniques such as yoga and meditation.

OBTAINING SUPPORT FROM OTHER STUDENTS

The best way to seek support from other students is to make friends with like-minded students on your course, especially adults who may be experiencing similar stresses and tensions. However, there are a number of other groups that can offer advice and support for you during your studies.

Local Student Support

The level of support for students in your college or university will depend upon the needs and requirements of students at your institution. If you find that you do not have any student support groups you could think about setting them up yourself. Many colleges and universities will have the following types of groups:

Mature Students' Society – this may be part of the Students' Union or it may have been set up independently by students at the college or university. Consult notice boards, ask at the Students' Union reception or consult your university website or prospectus for more information.

Informal Study Groups – many students set up informal study groups to help, support and encourage each other with their studies. Ask your tutor for more information.

Network Study Groups – on many campus networks there is space for students to exchange ideas and to support each other through their studies. Consult your Computer Services help desk or website for more information.

National Student Support

Two of the most useful organisations in the UK offering support, information, advice and guidance to adult students are the Mature Students' Union and the National Union of Students:

The Mature Students' Union (MSU) is an 'apolitical, self-funding campaign and support organisation dedicated to the equal inclusion of all students classified as mature'. It aims to promote the interests of mature students and to act on their behalf:

More information about the MSU can be obtained from their website:

www.msu.org.uk

The National Union of Students represents the interests of all students in the UK. Within the organisation is the Mature Students' National Committee which works closely with the Mature Students' Union:

The National Union of Students (NUS)

2nd Floor

Centro 3

Mandela Street

London NW1 0DU

www.nusonline.co.uk

SEEKING PROFESSIONAL HELP

If your studies are causing undue stress or anxiety and it is affecting your life in adverse ways, there are a number of people employed in colleges and universities to help you.

Welfare Services

Many college and university students' unions run an advice and welfare service for their members. As a student you can become a member of the students' union and you can use any of the services they offer free of charge. Many places will have a trained, permanent member of staff who can offer help and advice on any welfare issue. Some of these services will have a 'drop-in' session and others will offer an appointment service. Speak to the receptionist at your Students' Union for more information.

Counselling Services

Many universities employ their own student counsellor, and if they don't the welfare services will be able to put you in touch with a counsellor outside the college or university. Student counsellors specialise in dealing with the problems faced by students and some are available twenty-four hours a day, seven days a week. A counsellor's role is to offer support and understanding and to listen and respond in a non-judgemental, non-critical way. They help you to focus on, and understand more clearly, the issues that concern or trouble you.

University counselling services are free to students requesting counselling. When you contact the counselling service you will receive a brief exploratory interview to find out what will be the best way forward. Seeking counselling is not an admission of failure, weakness or inadequacy – it's about making a positive choice to get the help that you need (see Liz's example below).

For more information contact your college or university counselling service or consult the Heads of University Counselling Services website: www.student.counselling.co.uk

Medical Facilities

Most universities and some larger colleges have their own medical centre on campus. As a student you can register with a campus doctor when you begin your course. These doctors specialise in treating ailments and problems encountered by students and they will be able to refer you to other services outside the campus if required. Appointments with doctors and nurses can be arranged on campus and an emergency number is provided for evenings and weekends. Visit your medical centre to register.

Religious Services

Many universities and colleges have their own chaplain and religious advisers. These represent various faiths including Anglican, Roman Catholic, Methodist, Pentecostal, Buddhist, Hindu, Islam, Jewish and Sikh. Some will hold full-time appointments within the student community, others are part-time, having congregations elsewhere and welcoming students into their communities. Some colleges and universities invite in leaders of other denominations and/or provide prayer rooms for religious reflection and support. Most universities and some larger colleges have religious groups of various denominations set up by the students to offer services, social activities, comfort and support. Consult your university website or student services for more information.

Seeking Help – Student Case Studies

Adam (29)

I was having some personal problems at home. I've got a son who's three and very demanding. While my wife was at home she looked after him in the evenings when I went to study, but she left me and I was left with the problem of how to study and look after Luke. I just couldn't do it so I decided to leave my course. But I'd been doing really well and my tutor suggested I go and speak to a bloke in the Students' Union. He told me about the college nursery and also told me about hardship funds. He said he would help me make an application for the extra money and he would see about places in the nursery. I couldn't get a place in the nursery straightaway 'cos it was full, but we got Luke on the waiting list. The extra money came in really handy when I had to arrange for a babysitter or childminder. I carried on studying on my course, but I wouldn't have been able to do it if I hadn't spoken to that bloke.

Liz (41)

I went through a pretty rough patch what with one thing and another. My dad died, my children were having problems at school and I was feeling really, really guilty about trying to carry on with my course. But I was in my third year and I just couldn't waste everything I'd done. We are a close family and their grandpa dying really affected the children, especially with them not having a father. I'd talked to my dad about everything – it was him who encouraged me to do the course. Now he'd gone I'd got no one and I felt really lost and out of my depth. But I knew I *had* to finish my course and I *had* to help my children, so I talked to my tutor who told me about the counselling service. We've always kept problems in the family so I wasn't sure about talking to someone else. But I knew I had to do something, I was having terrible mood swings and it was affecting my children and my studies. Sometimes I felt so down I didn't want to get out of bed. So I went to the counselling service and had a chat. They told me they had someone there who specialised in bereavement counselling so I went to see her.

In the end I think I had six appointments, all for about an hour to two hours. I just spoke about my dad most of the time and why I missed him so much. Most times I would just burst into tears. But that was good 'cos I would never do that in front of my children. I always felt drained after the sessions and really tired, but so much better. They gave me some information on helping children to cope with bereavement. Then they helped me to talk through my studies, why I was doing it, what I wanted for me and the children. I look back on those sessions really fondly – I think they helped me to sort myself out in so many other ways. I would never, ever see needing counselling as a sign of weakness.

SUMMARY

As the above two examples have shown, seeking professional advice should not be seen as a sign of weakness. If you are finding it hard to cope with the pressure of study you may wish to look into what type of help is available at your college or university.

During some of my research with adult learners, some adults pointed out that it was the support that they had received from other students which had most helped them through their course. This support was especially significant for adults who had chosen to be residential students. They pointed out that friendships had developed between people because they had been able to understand the problems faced by each other. Many found that these friendships continued for many years after their courses had ended.

This chapter has provided advice on coping with the pressures of study. This includes seeking professional help, seeking informal support and recognising and coping with stress. Some adult students find that extra pressure is placed on them because of some actual or perceived problems with study. There are many services within colleges and universities that can help with these issues. These services are discussed in the next chapter.

18

Making the Most of Learner Support Services

Colleges and universities provide a wide variety of learner support services. The tutors and other staff at your institution want you to do well on your course and they will try to provide any extra services that will help you to succeed.

As a student you are entitled to use any of these services and most will be free of charge. The services have been set up for you and you should take advantage of them if you need to. This chapter provides information about these services.

HELP WITH STUDY SKILLS

Learner Support Unit

Many colleges and universities have a *Learner Support Unit* or *Study Skills Unit* that is available to help students with basic skills in reading, writing and numeracy. If you feel you are struggling with any of these skills, special sessions (to be held within these units) can be arranged outside your course timetable. In the unit you can access learning resources and materials, computing facilities and other technological aids. Advice from supportive, trained staff is also available when required.

At most institutions you will have a confidential interview with the learning support tutor who will discuss the problems you are facing, look at your strengths and weaknesses and find out about your hopes and fears. Together you will develop an individual learning plan which will lay out your aims and objectives, setting realistic goals for the short- and long-term. The learner support tutor will focus on information relevant to your course. This will make the support that you receive more interesting, relevant and useful. Some tutors will liaise with your course tutor to make sure that they give you the best possible help.

This type of learner support tends to be offered in an informal, workshop setting – you can either book a regular time to visit or drop into the unit. This can be useful when you need help with something that may be short-term and quite specific. The aim of these units is to give you the skills

---

Jim (42)

I have dyslexia. I was really concerned about going to university 'cos I thought I would have no chance with the reading and writing. My tutor told me about the Study Skills Unit and advised me to go and speak to someone there. I was worried that everyone on my course would call me thick, but I had to go 'cos I was even more worried about my coursework. The first thing that surprised me was the large amount of students who went there – all sorts of people – young, old, male, female. It made me realise I wasn't the only person with problems.

> The tutors helped me through my first year – they were really supportive and I wouldn't have been able to do it without them. They helped me to feel much more confident about what I could do. I don't have to go back but I do because I like going there and now I can help other new students. I found it so useful to get support off other students and now I'm doing it for other people. If you have any sort of problems with study skills I'd say go straightaway.

and confidence to move on in your studies until you no longer need the support of the unit.

Study Support Sessions

Many colleges and universities will offer study support sessions for students who would like extra help with study skills, such as essay writing, note-taking, presentation skills and revision techniques. A timetable of sessions is drawn up each semester. The sessions are free to students and you can choose which sessions you wish to attend. They are led by an experienced tutor and time may be set aside at the end of the session for individual students to raise questions. Ask your tutor, contact the college or university reception, or consult their website for more details.

SUPPORT FOR INFORMATION TECHNOLOGY

The IT equipment and services available will vary between institutions. However, most university and college Computing Services will provide some or all of the following:

- A campus network of PCs, some with 24-hour access.

- Workstations and laboratories.

- Advice and help desk service.

- Printing services.

- Electronic mail (e-mail).

- Network connection service.

- Audio visual equipment.

- Assistance and training in most/all aspects of information and communication technology, such as using e-mail, the internet, word processing packages and so on.

- Computer shop selling hardware and software at educational prices. These are special discounts worked out between hardware and software manufacturers and educational establishments. Generally, a wide range of specialist and commercial packages are available and staff will be able to offer good advice about what you might find useful. To purchase this equipment at discounted prices you will need evidence of your student status (usually your Students' Union card or your library card).

When you start college or university, visit the Computing Services department or consult their website. Staff will provide you with information sheets about the services on offer, including training courses and details about the help desk. They will set you up with an account for the central system and an e-mail account. Take advantage of all the free services and equipment offered by the university. Some staff might help you with any problems you have with your PC. Most Computing Services departments will produce information sheets and web pages that will help you diagnose problems yourself.

Remember that students studying on computing courses can be a very useful, free source of advice and information.

LEARNING RESOURCE SUPPORT

All colleges and universities have their own library which should contain most or all of the learning resources you need to successfully complete your course. Resources will vary between institutions, but in general you should have access to the following:

- Books
  - Reference books
  - Short loan collection
  - Standard loan
  - Inter-library loan

- Journals

- Exam papers

- Archives

- Document services

- Copying and binding

- Self-service copying and printing

- Factsheets

◆ Video and audio equipment

◆ Microfilm equipment

◆ Equipment for the visually impaired

◆ Access and visitor information

◆ Help desk

◆ Training courses on how to use databases, journals, etc.

The library catalogue will enable you to search the entire library stock using a variety of search techniques. It will show you in which building the publication is located and let you know whether it is out on loan. You can also use the library catalogue to check your own record of loans, self-renew your books and request other books.

When you begin your course make sure that you go on the library orientation tour as this is the best way to find out what is available. Consult your library website or speak to staff to find out what additional training is available.

In addition to using your own college or university library, you might wish to consider other options for more in-depth research. The British Library is the national library of the UK. The collection includes 150 million items with a further 3 million items incorporated every year. For more information consult their website: www.bl.uk.

COPAC is a service that gives free access to the online catalogues of 24 major university research libraries in the UK and Ireland, plus the British Library, the National

Library of Scotland and the National Library of Wales. Consult the website to access the service and to obtain more information: www.copac.ac.uk.

SUPPORT FOR STUDENTS WITH DISABILITIES

If you have a specific learning difficulty, such as dyslexia, or a physical health problem, such as poor eyesight, you should find out whether there is specialist help and support available. When you start your course, make contact with the **disability adviser** at your college or university. They are employed to help you with the following:

◆ Your applications for Disabled Students' Allowances (DSA). These are funds set up by the Government to help students with any extra costs you may have to pay as a result of your disability. The funds will pay for non-medical personal help, major items of specialist equipment, travel and other course-related costs. DSAs are not dependent upon your income.

◆ Arranging appointments for assessment of needs which are required for your DSA application.

◆ Helping put in place the support that is recommended.

◆ Liaison with the accommodation service and other university or college departments on your behalf.

◆ Supervising and arranging training for support workers.

◆ Providing help with special examination arrangements.

Library staff will provide a personal tour for people with disabilities so that they can assess your needs and any potential problems. Some libraries will provide staff who can offer one-to-one support throughout your course. Specialist equipment offered by your library may include:

◆ A PC with a large monitor, scanner and screen reading software.

◆ A Tieman Colour Reader which enlarges text and other images and displays them on a TV screen.

◆ A Kurzweil Personal Reader which scans text then speaks it out.

◆ Publications and instructions in Braille.

◆ A CleaReader audio text reader, which scans, stores and reads from books and other documents.

SUMMARY

Members of staff at colleges and universities want their students to succeed. To do this they will provide as many services as money and resources allow. As a student you should make the most of these services. This chapter has discussed the services that are most relevant to adult learners, including help with study support, information technology, learning resources and assistance for people with disabilties.

In this book advice and guidance has been offered on improving your study skills. Returning to learning can be a daunting process for adults. However, by reading this book and utilising available help you will find that your studies become enjoyable and successful. To conclude this book useful addresses and websites have been provided to help you further with your studies. I wish you every success and hope that you have found this book useful.

Useful Addresses and Websites

Adult Residential Colleges Association (ARCA)
6 Bath Road
Felixstowe
Suffolk IP11 7JW
01394 278161
www.arca.uk.net

This is the association of residential colleges for adult education. The colleges provide a wide range of short-stay courses for the general public.

Basic Skills Agency
7th floor
Commonwealth House
1–19 New Oxford Street
London WC1A 1NU
020 7405 4017
www.basic-skills.co.uk

The Basic Skills Agency is the national development agency for literacy, numeracy and related basic skills in England and

Wales. The agency defines basic skills as 'the ability to read, write and speak English and use mathematics at a level necessary to function and progress at work and in society in general'.

British Dyslexia Association
98 London Road
Reading
Berkshire RG1 5AU
0118 966 2677
www.bdadyslexia.org.uk

The British Dyslexic Association aims to be the voice of dyslexic people by enabling them to reach their full potential through creating a dyslexic-friendly society.

The National Institute of Adult Continuing Education
    (NIACE)
Renaissance House
20 Princess Road West
Leicester LE1 6TP
0116 204 4200
www.niace.org.uk

The National Institute of Adult Continuing Education (NIACE) is the national membership organisation for adult learning in England and Wales. The main aim of the institute is to promote the study and general advancement of adult continuing education.

The National Union of Students (NUS)
2nd Floor
Centro 3
Mandela Street
London NW1 0DU
0871 221 8221
www.nusonline.co.uk

The National Union of Students represents the interests of all students in the UK.

Skill: National Bureau for Students with Disabilities
Chapter House
18–20 Crucifix Lane
London SE1 3JW
020 7450 0620
www.skill.org.uk

Skill 'is a national voluntary organisation that aims to develop opportunities for people with disabilities and learning difficulties in post-16 education, training, employment and volunteering'.

The Age and Employment Network
207–221 Pentonville Road
London N1 9UZ
020 7843 1590
www.taen.org.uk

The Age and Employment Network is a campaigning organisation working with the media, employers and Government to change attitudes and public policies towards mature people who want to learn, work and earn.

Index